Working with the Dead

Working with the Dead

Josephine Price Powell

iUniverse, Inc.
New York Lincoln Shanghai

Working with the Dead

iUniverse, Inc.

For information address:
iUniverse, Inc.
2021 Pine Lake Road, Suite 100
Lincoln, NE 68512
www.iuniverse.com

The author has taken care to change the names of actual places or persons. Any resemblance of persons mentioned in the book to persons living or dead are purely coincidental.

ISBN: 0-595-31814-2

Printed in the United States of America

IN MEMORY OF MY LITTLE MOTHER
WHO ENCOURAGED ME EVERY STEP OF THE WAY.
GOD LOVE AND KEEP HER.

Contents

List of Characters

SONIA:	SHE HID HER PREGNANCY BY BINDING HER-SELF
JENNY:	MY LITTLE MOTHER
JEAN:	MY SISTER. WHO INTRODUCED ME TO JOHN
JOYCE:	MOTHER OF DEAD BABY (ON COUCH)
TED:	SONIA'S BROTHER
ROY:	EVIL LITTLE BASTARD
DORA:	SONIA'S MOTHER
BILL:	MY FATHER
ANNIE:	MY MOTHER
LOFTY:	SONIA'S HUSBAND
LITTLE PAUL:	BABY IN PRAM
ANNE:	DOLE MATE
CONNIE:	MY AUNT
SAMANTHA:	MY DAUGHTER
RONNIE:	AWOL TRUCKER
EDNA:	RONNIE'S WIFE
GEORGE:	LANDLORD OF SWAN PUB
NATHAN:	AMOROUS MANAGER
L J SCANDLANDS:	FIRST JOB IN FUNERAL SERVICE
BERT:	MANAGER AT SCANDLANDS
MAUREEN:	SCANDLANDS RECEPTIONIST

SIMON:	TRADE EMBALMER
FRED:	MY TEACHER
ROY:	EXAMINER (PRACTICAL EMBALMING)
SID WHITTLE:	SELF-MADE FUNERAL DIRECTOR
BIG FAT STINKING SLUG:	CALLED ME DR KILDARE!
ALLISON:	EMBALMER AND FRIEND
JOE:	ALLISON'S BOSS
LINDA:	MY COUSIN
JOAN:	LITTLE PETER'S MOTHER
DAVE:	MY HUSBAND
JACKIE:	WHO TAUGHT ME TO ARRANGE FUNERALS
PHYLLIS:	WITH THE SQUEAKY FAN BELT
DAN:	FAT BOY
DAVID:	A BORING STUDENT
PAM:	LADY WITH PLUM IN MOUTH
BOB:	ROTTEN TEETH
BRIAN:	LOOSE HEAD
JED:	SAID I WOULD MAKE A GOOD TEACHER
FRANK:	THE SPIKER
ALLEN:	EMBALMING EXAMINER (TEACHING EXAM)
BARBARA:	MY STUDENT
LITTLE THIMBLE FIST:	LITTLE DROWNED GIRL
PETER:	BABY IN CASKET (ON DRESSER)

PART ONE:

WORKING WITH THE DEAD

First encounter with Death

My first encounter with death was when I was about eight years old. A baby girl had died just a few doors up from us and I went with my mother to see her. The baby was lying on the couch, propped up on a very dirty pillow. Her nightdress was dirty too!

On the mantelpiece was a baby's bottle half filled with 'pobbies' (Bread and Milk). I heard quiet voices explaining what had happened. Apparently the child had choked to death after being left with her bottle banked up on a pillow. The lice leaving her body made the sight all the more ghastly. It was dreadful! My mother exchanged some harsh words with the baby's mother. The next day the mother accepted some of my doll's clothes for the baby to be buried in.

There was no doubt the child had been neglected for some time. In fact, there was a little bastard living in that baby's household called Roy. He was the same age as me—but he was evil! He would shove lollie-sticks up the baby's nose and smack its little face as he walked by.

On the day of the funeral the mother was booed by all the neighbours—not us, I hasten to add! She left the area and had seven more children—all boys.

I was to learn more about that 'house' and visit one more time to see Death. My mother told me the sister of the dead baby's mother had got herself pregnant. In those days it was looked upon as something very shameful to be carrying a Bastard child. My sister was also pregnant (married, however) with her first baby and 'Sonia' would go with her to the clinic. The Nurse would ask Sonia for her appointment card, but she would 'rear' up on them, adamantly stating she wasn't pregnant. My mother knew for a fact that she was and asked her outright, yet the answer remained 'no'—no doubt the girl was in a state of denial.

Sonia's mother Dora, who was built like a bull, came storming into our house and played hell with my mother. "Leave our Sonia alone!" she screamed. "She's *not* pregnant!"—and with that she waddled out of the door, nearly taking off its hinges.

However, there wasn't the slightest doubt in my mother's mind that Sonia was with child and that it would only be a matter of time before the truth was out—and when it did come out, the truth was far from pleasant.

Sonia's Deception

Sonia and her mother kept away from our house, but one morning before leaving for work, Sonia's brother Ted told her there was a 'bad stink' in the house and if it was still there on his return he was going to turn the house upside down until he 'found' the cause.

Sonia had, in fact, given birth in one of the bedrooms and never made a sound. The girl must have been as hard as nails! The child was a full term boy, but we will never know if it was born dead or alive.

Sonia begged her mother to help her get rid of the remains, which she had kept in a suitcase. Her mother duly helped her to do so—by throwing the remains on the fire!

Now, you may be thinking, 'Why weren't they prosecuted?' Well, for a start, there was no evidence that Sonia was ever pregnant; she had never seen a Doctor, and in any case it was a long time after the event that Dora blurted it all out to my mother.

Poor Lofty

I was fourteen when both my two brothers and sister left home, leaving just me, Jenny and my mother and father.

Jenny, now divorced, had three boys. She had suffered from rheumatic fever as a child, which left her with a weak heart. Her doctor was astounded that all three births had taken place without any complications, but she never mentioned her heart condition and did all of the things any fit person would do. Jenny's heart was never an issue in our family, though it must be admitted she could never run as fast as me!

Sonia was courting a dear friend of my father's, called Lofty. My father would exclaim, "Whatever possessed Lofty to take up with *her!*"

Sonia and Lofty married and lived with Dora, but things soon began to go wrong. Lofty would have the odd pint with my father and tell him about his lazy wife and her lazy mother; in short, Lofty was regretting ever tying the knot with Sonia—but unlike today, marriages then were usually 'until death do us part.'

Lofty wouldn't have long to wait! He became ill with stomach cancer and was confined to bed; refusing to go into hospital, he was to be cared for at home by his wife!

Sonia would come down to us and tell us that Lofty was getting weaker and hard work to look after. The trips down to our house were a break for her, and she told us that both she and her mother were taking turns caring for Lofty.

It was late one evening when the doorbell rang and on the doorstep was Lofty's brother. He asked for my father and I showed him in.

Lofty was dead and his brother was heartbroken, as it turned out. His brother had been up to the house to see him and was telling my father about him. Putting on his coat, my father didn't hesitate to tell him he would go and pay his respects—and I went with him.

I'll never forget what I saw—a long, skeletal-like figure prostrate on an old camp bed, wearing just the bottom half of his pyjamas. I could count every rib—there wasn't an ounce of flesh on his body, and covering each eye socket was a penny. And the smell was sickening—stinking bed, stinking room!

Standing close to my father I looked up at his face and saw he was struggling not to break down.

"Couldn't you have got him into hospital?" he asked the lazy wife, who almost snapped her reply that he would not go in.

We learned later that during Lofty's last days he would call out for Sonia for a drink of water, which was denied many times. She would walk out of the door when he was crying in pain. It was Dora who spilt the beans on Sonia who by then had gone to live with another man.

Paul

The next few months saw me occupied with my friend's horse. I had forgotten about the 'house of death' and was just having a great time. However, a friend of my mother had lost her little boy in a tragic accident.

Little Paul had been bursting tar bubbles outside his house when he was run over by a milk float. The driver failed to see the boy and reversed over him, killing him instantly.

Mother told me to go and take some flowers and to say that she would be along later that day. Paul's mum answered the door and I conveyed the message from my mother. I offered her the flowers, but she asked if I would like to 'bring' them in and turned to walk down the lobby. I followed and there was a large navy and white pram, with little Paul in it. He was dressed in a blue and white sailor suit, white ankle socks, little white boots; his little fat legs were in a relaxed position with his arms placed above his head.

"He looks like he's asleep," I whispered and his mother nodded in agreement. She gave me a smile, but I could see the sadness in her face. She must have been going through hell, but I was too young to comfort her. I said that my mother would be along soon and left.

◆　　　◆　　　◆

I will never forget those that I saw dead—the little one who choked on her pobbies, little Paul that had been loved so much, the new-born that had never been given the chance of life, and poor Lofty who had been left to die in agony.

As for me, I was then a teenager, ready to take on the world, full of zeal, and the last thing on my mind was 'Death'—though not for long. 'Death' was preparing to catch up with me again.

Growing out of Horses

Expelled from school at the age of fourteen, I was as happy as a lark. I was too headstrong for my teachers; they couldn't handle me, so they let me go, and I was enjoying every minute, going to fairs and caring for horses for a local horse dealer and getting paid for it!

I stuck with the horse trade till I was nineteen and then decided I wanted a change, so I got a job in a factory; but I wasn't happy getting out of bed in the middle of winter at 7.00am, nor clocking in and being 'locked in' till 5.00pm. God, how I hated it! I had a friend who was in the same mind as me, and we would flit from job to job, never lasting long after the first pay packet. We got good at going for interviews and giving the 'wrong' impression: they would usually end up ticking the box on the green card as 'unsuitable'.

I spent more time in the dole queues than at home! Inevitably the 'signing' on day came and my friend and I set off. Now, if you didn't keep the appointment you didn't get paid, and for some reason on that day I was drawn to my Aunt Connie's house—not that I ever visited her, but for some reason I felt compelled to go.

My friend Anne reminded me of the consequences, but to no avail. I told her to go on and that I would meet up with her later.

On reaching Connie's I found the front door open. I tapped gently on the middle door and heard a frail voice telling me to 'come in'.

There she lay on the bed, the room darkened on account of the thick heavy curtains that were drawn to. I walked over and sat beside her. She was a woman of about 56, but looked older, having been in and out of hospital for one ailment after another. I asked if I could open the curtains but she said no. She became agitated but said how glad she was that I had come. Pointing to the floor, she asked me to get her bag from beneath the bed and take from it a large brown envelope.

She explained that on no account must it be given to anyone but her son (when I found him!). I took the envelope and put it in my bag—and within the next minute her brother Barry walked in. Completely ignoring me, he asked Connie how she was, but she didn't answer. I told him I was just passing and that I needed to sign on. Reaching under the bed for the bag, he said, "I have to get back to work." (Where does that leave me, I thought!) Tucking the bag under his arm, he turned to Connie and said he would get back later. (Dick!)

We were on our own now and I reassured Connie that her son would get the envelope. Then she became restless and said she needed the toilet. There was no way she could make the stairs. There was a bucket in the back so I went for it. Trying to get Connie off her bed was like moving a plank of wood, she was so stiff. Eventually I got her over the bucket. The fire was high and I was beginning to sweat; the muscles in my arms started to ache and I was praying for her to finish.

Connie's Passing

Eventually I got Connie back to bed and suggested she put on her nightie. I helped her with it, but she wouldn't get into bed; instead, she went to the bedhead and held onto the rails, saying she was falling. She began asking for her mother who, incidentally, had been dead for some time. That's when I really began to worry.

By this time Connie had a tight grip of my hand. I felt I'd better call her doctor, so I pretended I needed to buy some fags. (Come to think of it, I *did* need a fag!) Once outside I phoned her GP who came out and examined her back and front.

I was holding her up (again) and the GP was babbling on about her going into hospital, but Connie refused. He started for the door and, dragging myself out of Connie's grip once again, I followed the GP down the street. I told him I thought Connie was dying. He stood for a moment and said he would get an ambulance out as soon as he could.

I flew back to Connie and coaxed her into bed, telling her to try and get some sleep. I was feeling somewhat weary now, not to mention skint! I mulled over the problem of who I could get hold of to take over, but it wasn't to be, for once again Connie took my hand in hers and said, "You are my Angel."

Connie never spoke again but slipped into a deep sleep, and I knew I wasn't going anywhere—at least not until she was dead.

She died about five minutes before the ambulance arrived. I told them she had gone, but they tried to resuscitate her anyway—then someone turned on the light! God! She looked dreadful. Her face was like a little wax doll. She had bruises all over her body.

She was buried pretty quickly, as within a couple of days she had gone black! I didn't attend the funeral. Her brother came to see me, asking for the 'envelope'. He called me a thief and threatened me with violence, but nothing came of it. I smile to myself still, recalling the sight of him dashing off with Connie's bag under his arm, thinking he had got the 'booty'!

The brown envelope contained a will and some documents that were connected to some savings; there was also some paper money, and I delivered it all to her son.

John

Two years after my Aunt Connie's demise I was still in and out of jobs, but things were about to change—and so was my life.

One afternoon my other sister Jean came over from Blackpool to see me. We went into a pub called The White Bull and there—standing at the bar—was a man much older than me and I loved him at first sight!

I asked my sister if she knew him and, unfortunately or fortunately for me, she did, and advised me to keep away from him. "His name is John," Jean said, "and he is a Mr *Crunch*" (she spoke the name with emphasis!). It was too late: I asked her to bring him over to our table. I was twenty-one, he was forty-three! Married, too, with a grown up family—but we were inseparable! I began drinking heavily, upsetting my family and his, but I didn't care. Drinking sprees could last a week, sleeping where we could—it didn't matter as long as we were together.

By the time I was twenty-five I was pregnant with twins. Sadly, I lost one at birth, which had nothing to do with my lifestyle. (Believe it or not, as soon as I knew I was pregnant I stopped drinking and smoking for the duration of my pregnancy.) I called my baby Samantha Jayne, and in effect it was she who saved my life, for without her I would have more than likely ended up an alcoholic. John did, though, and as much as I loved him, he had to go. He just seemed to disappear from my life as quickly as he entered it—God bless him.

I was happy at home with Samantha. My father had passed away but my mother was good to me. In spite of all I had put her through, she gave me all the support I needed. But money was scarce and I needed to work. Fortunately, a night job came up at a factory near my home. The pay was good and I was with

Samantha during the day. One of my workmates, Edna, became a good friend. I would call round at her house at weekends and style her hair. We always had a good laugh and she would give me few bob. Then her husband Ronnie, a long distance lorry driver, was to do something completely out of character!

Ronnie Goes AWOL

It was Monday evening and Edna didn't turn up for work. I called at her house on the way home and found her sitting in front of the fire. I could see she'd been crying. She told me Ronnie had left her! She showed me the note he had shoved through the letterbox. I thought it was strange, for Ronnie certainly wasn't a womaniser. Nevertheless Edna thought he had gone off with another woman. I had to leave but told her to keep in touch.

The next day she phoned and asked me to come round. When I arrived Ronnie was seated in the chair, his head in his hands. I sat quietly opposite. He lifted his head and asked for the curtains to be drawn. The daylight was hurting his eyes; the pain in his head, he said, was unbearable.

"Edna," I said, "you better ring an ambulance!"

Ronnie was rushed into hospital—he had suffered a massive brain haemorrhage and slipped into a coma. He never recovered.

Edna attached herself to me like a leech! She wouldn't go to the hospital without me, and when we did go there was nothing to do but sit and wait. He died a week later and the surgeon asked if they could do a hospital PM (Post Mortem—the family has to give permission for this kind of PM). I told Edna to say no, but she said if it would help someone else, then go ahead—and they certainly did.

Edna wanted Ronnie home—he was to repose in the front room under the window. She said she would send the kids to her mother's, and she and I would stay in the house with Ronnie. Nice one! I didn't want any of this, but I couldn't get out of it! My mother felt so sorry for Edna that she told me to stay with her until the funeral. Christ! They hadn't brought him home yet and it was going to be at least a week before the event.

I wasn't looking forward to it at all but I was all that Edna had so I gritted my teeth and waited for the 'homecoming.'

The night before Ronnie was brought home we went across the road to the Pub. She gave me the money for the drinks and we talked about Ronnie. We came to the conclusion that there had been something wrong with his mind that caused him to act in such a strange way. She said that when he returned he didn't have a clue where he had been and he was dead before he could remember!

Edna kept buying the drinks and every so often she would shove a pound note down the front of my blouse. By the time I walked out of the Pub I looked like Dolly Parton!

The booze began to take effect on Edna. In tears, she would lean on my shoulder and say, "We'll look after him, won't we, love?" I would smile and nod my head, but I wasn't looking forward to 'looking after Ronnie.'

Ronnie Arrives Home

We made our way back to Edna's and a few drinks later we decided to turn in. I shared Edna's bed and as soon as her head touched the pillow she was out like a light. Not so me—I kept thinking about Connie and how she looked, and hoped Ronnie wouldn't look like her! Eventually sleep overtook me. I slept till 8.00 the next morning when I was awakened by the phone. A voice from the funeral home said they would arrive at 9.30, which gave me and Edna some breathing space and time to prepare.

We busied ourselves sorting out the front room. Edna decided to make a brew and, whilst in the back, the hearse drew up at the door.

I called for Edna who came out of the kitchen with a frightened look on her face. "It's okay, Edna, everything will be okay," I reassured her, just as the FD (Funeral Director) knocked on the middle door. Edna gestured to me to let him in. I told him where we wanted the coffin and with that he summoned two of his staff who placed the coffin under the window. One of them removed the lid.

Ronnie was wearing a brown smoking jacket piped with a gold braid, but his head was wrapped in a large bandage! You couldn't see much of his face and Edna was later to say he looked like Lawrence of Arabia!

He didn't look good at all. His face was like alabaster, and his dark eyes gave away the pain he had suffered. Personally I would not have let anyone see him like that, but it was nothing to do with me.

I had the job of showing people in to pay their respects. The room was full of flowers and large candles burned brightly, two at either end of the coffin. Ronnie was Catholic, as were many who came to see him. I would leave them alone in prayer, and afterwards they would come in and sit for awhile with me and Edna and give me praise for all I was doing. I was wishing that one of them would change places with me! Indeed, every time the doorbell rang I would walk through 'Ronnie's room' and never looked at his coffin. It goes without saying that I took particular care not to look at him!

There was no going out that night. Edna wanted to stay in with Ronnie, so she opened a bottle of scotch. I paced myself out, but Edna went over the top! She was scared to death of that coffin. It was just me, Edna and Ronnie—two of us drinking and one of us dead quiet.

I was thinking about Samantha. I did so want to go home, but I couldn't leave Edna who by this time was quite pissed. "Come on, Jo," she said, staggering up on her feet. "I want to talk to Ronnie." I reached his door and told her to go in. "I'm just here," I told her. "You're okay."

She was hanging over the coffin side, blubbering and talking a lot of rubbish—but my heart went out to her. After a while I helped her to bed and she crashed out.

I finished what was left of the scotch. It had given me a little courage to check that everything was secure. I put the main lights on in you know whose room and extinguished the candles; finally, I checked the front door and not once did I look at the coffin. I climbed in next to Edna who was well away and I drifted into oblivion.

Someone's Outside!

It was early morning, about 3.00am, when I woke up wanting a pee—but the toilet was in the back yard! I prodded Edna and woke her up.

"I need a pee," I whispered.

She was quite coherent, considering she was totally pissed a few hours before.

"Yal have to go down yard," she said.

"Down yard!" I exclaimed in a loud whisper.

"*Shush*," she said. "I can here summat!"

That was the yard out for this girl, I can tell ya!

"What's it sound like?" I whispered. My eyes must have looked like organ stops!

"Like someone moving about downstairs," came the reply.

Ho Jesus, what had I got myself into! "Don't talk bloody daft!" I snapped. "There's no one down there." But Christ, I thought, there *was*—Ronnie! And I still wanted to pee!

It was no use—I *had* to go down. Once in the back kitchen I looked around and under the sink was an old washbowl. This was what I would have to use. I lifted my nightie and pulled my knickers to one side. What a relief! Any longer and I think I would have exploded. Keeping one eye on Ronnie's room, my water kept coming.

Without warning there was a loud knock on the back door! It made me jump and, letting go of my knickers, I flew up to Edna, jumped into bed and babbled out, "There's someone outside!"

"Put my dressing gown on and see who it is!" she said.

"No way, *you* go," I said, "and by the way, I peed in your washbowl."

We went down together. Edna shouted, "Whose there?"

"Police, Edna," came the reply.

I was getting rid of the 'bowl' contents and thinking, first name terms, huh? And there, in the doorway, stood two coppers to whom I took an instant dislike.

"We saw the light on and just wondered if you were all right," one of them said.

Like hell, I thought. These two toe rags were on the sniff! Out came the bottle and I took a drink. The two coppers had blown it! They hadn't counted on me being there, but they got the message and left.

After that night we stayed downstairs, all lights blazing with music playing till we fell asleep. All went well on the day of the funeral and I didn't see much of Edna afterwards, but one of the coppers did—regularly!

Factory Job Folds

Work at the factory was coming to an end and I needed to be 'earning'. It was on a rare night out with Jenny that events in my life took another turn.

It happened in the Swan pub. George, the Landlord, a large gentle giant, was asking for volunteers to 'give' a song. I liked George and offered to start the night off. It was great! The punters started coming in and George gave me a regular spot every Saturday night which paid £3.00.

One Saturday we were approached by a guy who asked if I would like to join his group as their 'girl singer'! The venue was at The Ship in the Dock area of Preston. Great, I thought! That was the area I was born in! I accepted his offer and reluctantly said goodbye to George.

I was having a good time at The Ship. The money was good and we were packing them in. A yacht had berthed in port. She was the *Dervish*, sailing round the world, and had stopped in Preston for repairs. Her crew plus reporter were regular visitors and I had an article written about me in the local paper. The truth is, however, that I really didn't like singing: I only saw it as a way of making money for Samantha and me, and things were going to get better.

Jenny saw an advert asking for a resident girl singer in the Mecca ballroom. "Go for it, Jo!" she urged. "You have a great voice." I pondered for a while, and then asked, "When are they Auditioning?" "Two o'clock tomorrow," came the reply.

One-thirty next day Jenny and I set of to 'Mecca' in my nineteen bow and arrow 'moggie'. When we arrived, there were plenty girls lined up waiting to give it their all and dressed to kill! I wore a white blouse and Levi jeans. Well, I hadn't auditioned before, and I didn't know one had to get dressed up like a Doll.

Jenny and I sat through what can only be described as painful; some were okay, but most of them apparently thought they could get by on boobs, thigh length boots and hair pieces.

Before long it was my turn. I only had two numbers—'Rose Garden', and the other—wait for it!—'I don't know why I love you but I do.' Afterwards the bandleader told us he would be in touch within the week to let us know who was in. The very next day I received a phone call: "We would like to offer you the residency, Jo."

My first week's wage was £25. I flew home with it and threw it into the air! Mother and Jenny screamed with delight! It looked like I was throwing confetti. I had never been paid so much for making a sound!

I stayed with 'Mecca' for two years, during which time I met my husband Dave. Once again I was to move onto something better. I started looking in Music papers and answered an advert in London. I didn't get the job I went for, but was asked if I would record demos for a record producer. I loved it, and eventually released my first record! Unfortunately it didn't get off the ground and my manager was becoming a little too fond of me. I wanted to get back to my roots, but I tried to stick with it, touring and finally ending up at the Royal Albert hall. Quite an achievement for a Lancashire lass!

Leaving London

Nevertheless, as I said, I wanted to get back to my roots and was soon on my way back home, with very little money and no job. My manager had tried to keep me, but I just couldn't hold on, I was so homesick.

Dave and I set to getting a cabaret act together. I was going on the road solo. This would be my job for the next fifteen years! Christ, how I hated it—but it gave us a good living, and then one day out of the blue, as I sat having lunch with Dave, a voice spoke to me. Now you may think I had 'lost' it, but believe me, I heard it—a male voice in my head, which quietly said: "Change direction—go into the Funeral service."

By this time Dave had left the table and was reading a paper. I turned and said, "Dave, I'm going to change direction." As men do, he just gave a grunt which meant he'd heard me, though I doubt that he had.

I went into my little study and started looking through the phone book for Funeral services. I had no doubt in my mind that this is what I had to do, but the way I got into the funeral profession is quite extraordinary.

To begin with, I selected three different Funeral businesses that I would approach. I was going to go and speak to them and tell them I would like to work in the profession. I couldn't take the chance on a phone call or a letter—I wanted them to see me in person. I knew I would have to pull all the stops out to succeed. I was excited about the prospect of going for a job that until an hour ago would never have entered my head; but entered my head it had and I had to see it through.

I went back to Dave and began telling him what my intentions were. This time he was listening!

"What about your bookings?" he asked. He looked at me, clearly surprised.

"I'll carry on singing, but I'll choose my venues," I replied with confidence.

Dave would never stand in my way. He knew that once I had made my mind up, that was it; and he also knew I would never put us in a position that would leave us financially embarrassed.

I didn't tell Dave about the voice, but something had changed in me. I was not the same woman he had just dined with. I felt as if I had been waiting for something to happen to take me out of the trap I had put myself in, and it had!

Monday morning arrived and I was up early, getting a shower, then looking in my wardrobe for something suitable to wear. I chose a grey suit and white blouse and wore very little make-up. I was ready to go, so taking one last look in the mirror, I said so long to Dave and marched off.

The previous night in bed I had it all 'sussed out'—what I was going to say and how I would present myself; but now it didn't feel as simple! What would they make of me? I began to wonder whether once they found out what I did for a living they'd lose interest! Best not to mention anything, I thought. I would just say that I was a housewife with no ties and looking for a part-time job in the funeral service—just like that. No, it didn't sound right, but I was nearly at my first point of call, so there was no turning back now!

Scandlands Funeral Service

The sign above the door read Scandlands Funeral Service, and what a place it was—an old Victorian building that had seen better days, but still Majestic. I walked into the reception and asked for the manager. He was young and very pleasant and invited me into his office. His name was Bert and he asked how he could help me.

I told him what I thought he would like to hear and he was kind enough to listen; and then he asked me if I would like a look around. We toured the offices, garage, canteen and then the grand staircase. The staircase was magnificent, each stair covered with a deep red carpet. As the stairs rose they swept round into a panelled corridor. I commented on the size of the building and the grand staircase and Bert said it was one of the last of its kind. Lining the corridor were doorless rooms, each curtained-off with drapes as red as the carpet.

"These are rest rooms," Bert said. Pulling back one of the curtains, he showed me in. There was some kind of wooden trestle against the wall that I took for a support for a coffin, an easy chair in the corner, while a little corner table held an empty flower vase.

"They're all the same," Bert said, "but the one I'm going to show you next is much grander."

It was, too—more like a chapel. It boasted a large oak-panelled door and inside was lavishly decorated. Bert went on to tell me that this was for the young and the clergy, and indeed those that wanted more room in which to sit and pay their respects. The other rest rooms were mainly for the old and those that had no family or very few visitors. He went on to say that services were sometimes held in the oak panelled room.

We then carried on through another door which led into a lift. When it was at its highest elevation one could walk through to the other side and into the 'Coffin shop'. In there were boxes of shroud, small coffins, large coffins and baby caskets. As I was looking around he asked me if I was okay. I nodded a 'yes'. Bert apologised for the nude calendars on the wall and said not many women came up there.

"This door leads into the mortuary," Bert continued. Following him in, I was taken by the size of it. It resembled a very large kitchen with worktops and cupboards, but instead of pots and pans there were instruments lying on the top of the units; and on the tiled floor were four porcelain slabs, each with a channel running through the middle interrupted by a drain hole, under which was a metal bucket. "This is where we embalm," said Bert. He showed me a machine, with tubes leading from it to a container of pink fluid. I was to learn later that this was an embalming chemical. Next to the 'sluice' for bodily fluids was a toilet without a board or lid! I was assured by Bert that the drainage in this room was separate for the domestic. Good job, I thought.

I wanted to see more, but Bert looked at his watch and moved over to a very large walk-in fridge. "I'll not open it," he said. "There's a body in, but it's quite a mess, so I think we'll leave our tour here." I agreed, but I knew I was hooked! I mentioned again that I would come for free to gain some experience. Bert smiled and asked me if I would like a coffee.

There was nothing for me at the moment, Bert said, but he took my number and said he would keep in touch.

Then something very strange happened.

I'm In!

I was just about to drive out of Scandlands courtyard, considering my next port of call, when, looking through my rear-view mirror, I saw Bert waving his arms and gesturing me back. Getting out of my car I walked towards him.

"Come back in the Office," he said, "I think I may have something for you."

Great, I'm in, I thought! Bert went on to say it would be part-time in the office, but at least it would be a start; he had a secretary called Maureen who would 'show' me the ropes, and he asked if I would like to come in next Monday.

I thanked Bert sincerely and made my way back home, striking the other two services from my list. Dave, as usual, was happy for me to do my little part-time job and I had every intention of making the funeral profession my career.

Monday came and I was outside Scandlands before anyone else. This time I was in a black suit complemented by a starched white blouse, black stockings and shoes. I didn't have to wait long before a woman drove up and parked her car next to mine. She wasn't young, but I took her to be 'Maureen'. I was right. "Are you Jo?" she asked. I answered with a quiet 'yes'.

I followed her into the office and she began looking through the mail. Indicating a chair opposite her desk, she bade me sit and began asking me what kind if office work I had done! "Not much," I replied, "but I can type." She didn't know who she was addressing! I was a professional singer, not a pen pusher; but although set in her ways, Maureen was to be instrumental in my fast approaching embalming career and we became firm friends.

Things could get quite hectic at Scandlands and I was learning the 'ropes' pretty quickly. Maureen knew the job inside out and was a good teacher, and although she didn't mention it, I think she enjoyed having me there. One particular morning Maureen was waiting for a family to arrange the funeral of their daughter who had been killed in a road accident. Her time had been taken up with this family and the arrangements were proving quite difficult. "If anyone comes to see Mr Parry, Jo, take them up—you know what to do."

Of course I knew what to do. Maureen had drummed it into me that a body had to be 'checked' before taking anyone in to see it. "Things can go wrong," she had warned—just what could go wrong was something I intended to make her elaborate on when I had the time.

It wasn't long before the bell rang in reception. I could see a little old man, cap in hand, waiting to be attended to. I went out to him and asked if I could help.

"'Av cum ta see Mr Parry," was the reply.

"Would you care to go up in the lift?" I asked the frail old man.

"All be o' reet so long as a tek mi time."

God, he spoke broader than me! We slowly ascended the stairs and he sat down outside the rest room. I told him I would turn on the lights for him and disappeared behind the curtain. There was Mr Parry, his face covered by a cowl. I knew I had to lift it away but I started to think about Aunt Connie. What if Mr Parry's face was like hers?

But it wasn't. He looked at peace, so I showed the old man in. He said he had been a lifelong friend to Mr Parry who had "a long stocking"; though he was quite miffed that his pal hadn't left him the price of a pint, he took out his handkerchief and wiped a tear from his eye. I just said in my softest voice, "Never mind."

"Aye, never mind," he repeated after me. He thanked me and I showed him out.

Poor man.

The Trade Embalmer

Back in the office I was looking at Maureen over the desk. I wanted to know more about the 'things' that can go wrong, and I asked her. She said that some bodies 'leak' after they've been placed in their coffin and this will stain the gown; consequently we need to make sure that we check the body before showing anyone in to view. Now Maureen wasn't an embalmer and to push her any further would have been useless, but I wanted more information—and there it was walking in through the office door: 'The trade embalmer'.

Simon—that was his name—embalmed Scandlands' bodies. Maureen introduced me to him. I made him a 'brew' and he started asking me about my job; I wanted to know about *his*, of course, but the time wasn't right—he had to 'get on' so I would have to wait.

Once Simon was out of the room I began to 'pump' Maureen about him. She told me that he could embalm a body in twenty minutes! But within a couple of days, apparently, they 'go off'.

"Go off?" I queried, alarmed.

"Why, yes," she replied. "They begin to deteriorate and smell! He doesn't spend enough time on them." She could see I was hanging on every word and leant over to reach a switch at the side of her desk. "Can Jo come up and watch you, Simon?" she asked.

"Send her up," was the reply.

Off I went at full speed, but stopped abruptly outside the mortuary door. I began to ask myself if I was up to this, as my idea of embalming was cotton wool balls and cosmetics! I was soon to learn that there was a lot more to it than that! I knocked on the door and a voice said 'enter.'

What a sight met my eyes! There, on one of the slabs, was a body that had been subjected to a post mortem examination. From where I was standing, with both hands cupped over my mouth, I could see into the back of the head! The top of the skull had been removed and so had the brain—so the head was just an empty cavity! The body's trunk was laid open and Simon was removing the internal organs, placing them at the bottom of the slab. It was just a blaze of red against the stark white of the slab, and trying to ignore the stench I moved closer.

"Put a gown on, Jo." Simon pointed to a locker at the far end of the room. "There are some wellies you can wear and some rubber gloves." I just stared at the locker and went into automatic pilot. Garb on, I asked if I could do anything. "Yes," came the reply, "bring me a bucket and a bottle of the green stuff on top of one of the units." He picked up the internal organs and placed them carefully in the bucket and asked me to pour the 'green stuff' (which was cavity fluid) over them. It was strong stuff and my eyes began to run. Cavity fluid disinfects the internal organs, I was told, and formaldehyde is used to sanitise the rest of the body. I was looking at the gore in the bucket—liver, intestines, parts of the brain that had been incised for examination. Not a pretty sight for a rookie, but I was compelled to stay.

Simon told me there were two kinds of cases. One was 'straight' and the other 'PM' (Post Mortem).

The embalmer replaces the body's blood with formaldehyde to preserve and restore the body. He showed me arteries in the neck of the corpse and said this was where one inserted the embalming chemical. He placed a curved metal tube into the artery and clamped it to prevent it from slipping out; the metal tube had a long rubber tube attached to it and this led to a large plastic container which contained the formaldehyde.

I Want to be an Embalmer

Simon turned on a switch and embalming fluid began to flow. He told me to look into the back of the head of the corpse. He had placed two little clamps inside the skull. These would prevent fluid loss into the brain cavity. Then he told me to watch the face, and indeed the colour was changing from a deathly grey to a warm pink. I was mesmerised.

Simon sent the chemical through both arteries in the neck; he did the same with the arteries in each arm and the legs. Simon gave me a suction pump and told me to aspirate the trunk cavity. I felt like I was doing something very important.

All done, Simon 'dusted' the cavities with some powder; he then placed some wadding in the neck area and in the pelvic area. The internal organs were transferred to a strong plastic bag and replaced into the trunk cavity. Simon stitched the incision in the trunk and then showed me how to put back the top of the skull. He took some wadding about the same size as a brain and placed it in the brain's cavity. He then put back the top of the skull, and bringing both ends of the scalp together he secured it with stitches. The corpse was then washed, features set and the hair shampooed and dried.

I must say that there was a distinct change from when I first saw the body. I enjoyed every minute watching Simon and doing my bit, and I knew that I had to be an embalmer.

The buzzer went. I was needed and I wanted so much to ask Simon how he became an embalmer, but I had to go. Maureen had let me stay long enough, but I needn't have worried, for it was Maureen who was to point me in the right direction.

Becoming an Embalmer

Back in the office Maureen asked how I had got on. "Great," I replied. "I would like to learn!"

She smiled and said she knew someone who could teach me. True to her word, she introduced me to an Embalming Teacher and I enrolled in his class. I never missed a session and passed all theory exams with flying colours. He gave me every opportunity to embalm and I was soon learning how to recognise a bad embalming from a good one. I was being taught by the best and I will always be in his debt.

It was the middle of June and very hot and I wasn't looking forward to pushing a pen in a stuffy office, but for the time being that is how it had to be. Maureen was just making a brew and I trotted off to do my 'checks'. Before I reached 'the curtain' I could smell something that turned my stomach! I had no choice but to go in. The body was green! Black parted lips made the corpse look as if it were smiling at me! God, the gown was soaking with a dark brown stain and it hummed to high heaven. This had to be one of Simon's specials.

I called down for a casual worker who automatically brought up a fresh gown and cotton wool. The poor sod had been here before and I was annoyed that he, or me, for that matter, should have to put right Simon's shoddy work.

We did what we could to the body and placed plenty of odour blocks in and around the coffin, and turning the lights low, we left.

Still angry, I made it clear to Maureen how I felt; but it wasn't the first time and she didn't seem that concerned.

"I told you what Simon's like," she said.

That's right, I thought she had. I found out that Simon was 'self taught', which means he never qualified with an embalming school. Not that all self-taught embalmers are bad—they're not. I know some very good ones, but to prevent bad habits being learnt, it would be wise to get a qualification from a good embalmer.

As far as the green body was concerned, no one came to view—thank the Lord.

As for Simon, well, he was cancelled out and Fred and I did Scandlands' bodies. Fred had put me in for my practical Exam and I was nervously waiting for the call to go. It came and I nearly threw my breakfast up! I wanted to pass so much, I had worked so hard, and I had got everything ready, even down to my bucket and sponge—and then they cancelled! They did it twice, so you can imagine the state of my nerves! But eventually I was on the road to Branigans Funeral service where my examiner was waiting.

My Practical Exam

On my arrival at Branigans I was met by a jolly chap who helped me in the back way with my equipment. The mortuary was small but adequate and I was asked to get ready.

I donned my protective clothing and set out my stall, so to speak, and waited for my examiner, who was a young man called Roy. The jolly chap wheeled in a trolley upon which was the case I had to embalm! Roy instructed me to proceed as if he wasn't there, and that's easier said than done! I went through the legal requirements and did the three tests for Death. So far so good. Removing the sheet from the body and placing a modesty cloth over the private parts, I observed that the condition of the body wasn't good.

She was a woman of eighty-nine, rather large in build and had been dead for about four days. She was a 'straight' case, which means the embalmer has to find the arteries he wants to inject into by surface projection, and I decided to raise an artery in her arm. I also needed to find a vein so I could relieve the body of its blood, the only fluid I wanted in being formaldehyde. I needed to hold my artery tube in place, so I reached for my suture—but there was only a couple of inches on it. I felt my face turning scarlet and nervously said, "Sorry, I must have brought the wrong spool." Roy didn't speak—he just gave me another from a cupboard, and he also wrote something down! Ho Christ, I thought, what's he written?!

Artery secured, I went for a vein in the leg. Having located it and got the vein tube in and secured, I was ready to roll. I would now turn on my machine and pump formaldehyde around the body.

Not a flicker came from my machine! I began to shrink inside and blurted out that it had never let me down before. Roy looked at me, and this time I detected he was a little bit miffed. Nevertheless I found the fault and replaced the fuse! (In silence, I might add.). *Please work*, I said under my breath, and the fluid began to flow.

I watched the old lady change before my eyes. The discoloration in her face began to clear, her skin becoming a subtle pink—her hands, too. I was in control of the situation! Filled with emotion, I felt I was taking away the years and pain—she did indeed look so much better and peaceful. Roy was still writing but I knew I was doing a good job.

Body saturated with fluid, I finished off and Roy handed me the lady's wig.

"You put it on, Jo," he said.

"I was going to do it later," I said.

"Never, mind—go on," he smiled.

I gave the wig a brush and placed it gently on her head. The difference was remarkable! She looked lovely and I was so glad he let me do it. He handed me a sheet and I covered her up to her chin and smiled at him. I choked up and he said, "Let's go for a cup if tea."

Six weeks later I received a call from Fred. "Congratulations, Jo, you've passed."

Happy as a Lark

Happy as a lark I flew into the office to tell Maureen the good news. Fred was on holiday for two weeks, so Simon was back. His bodies were going off after a couple of days, and visiting families were not complaining. Then it struck me that the Funeral Director would deal with them. Of course, that had to be it! Some can come up with some good excuses as to why a body is smelly. In fact, there was an incident when a family commented about "a smell coming from the coffin." The funeral director replied, "Well, that's your mother's way of saying it's time to close the coffin." Good one!

The funeral business is not all doom and gloom. There are some funny moments, but I hasten to add they are not directed to the deceased. I believe that if we do a good job and the families have a lasting peaceful memory of their loved ones, then we are entitled to a chuckle from time to time.

An old friend of mine who was a funeral director told me a story about a young apprentice that he had taken out on a 'removal.' It was a bitterly cold night and they were making their way to a remote farmhouse on the moors. The hearse slid its way to the front door where one of the farmhands stood holding a 'storm lamp'. The apprentice, a strong lad with a mop of flaming red hair, must have wanted to impress his boss. He strode up and asked in the deepest voice he could muster: "Where's the body?"

"Upstairs in bed," came the reply.

Both he and the FD made their way up the very narrow staircase with the stretcher.

The FD had been hoping the body wouldn't be too big, but no such luck. The body, sprawled out on the bed, was the farmer and built like a bull! Getting him onto the stretcher was no easy task, and manoeuvring him down the narrow stairs would be no easier. Quietly instructing his apprentice to secure the straps around the corpse, the lad was struggling in the dim light, but finally the straps were snapped in place.

The farmhand went ahead and held open the front door. The howling wind and rain smashing against the windows created an eerie scene for this removal. The FD told the lad to keep close to the wall and as near to the middle of the stretcher as he could. The FD held on to the back, afraid of it sliding out of his grip. Then they began the descent, but one of the straps had come loose and the arm of the corpse flopped over the side of the stretcher, the hand landing in the apprentice's hair!

"He's got me!" the lad screamed, and letting go of the stretcher bolted through the open door. The farmhand was obliged to take over.

The poor lad had taken refuge in the hearse, visibly shaken. The FD forgave him, nevertheless, and said he would see him the next day—but in fact never saw him again!

Trade Embalming

Scandlands had been condemned and I advertised that I was available to embalm 'free lance'. In the meantime I had been asked to look after a little funeral office owned by a self-made Funeral Director. What a man he was, foul mouthed and ripping everyone off that he came in contact with! I was determined to become acquainted with every side of the so-called caring profession and this was one side not to be missed.

The FD was called Sid Whittle and every other word he uttered began with 'F'. He talked about bodies as though they were pieces of meat. He laughed when telling me about a body that he had transported in the back of his car, covered with a blanket. "A wur friten ta deeth at blanket slippin' off it"—and he thought the next thing he told me even funnier. He had brought two bodies into his premises. There was very little room in his mortuary, so he put one body on the floor and the other on top; before leaving, he shouted to them: "No f—g while I'm away!"

I wanted to jump up and smack him in the mouth. Something told me he would not be the only lowlife I would encounter, and I was right.

I didn't stay long with Sid, but long enough to buy his embalming equipment, and I was ready for the road!

Thankfully it wasn't long before the phone began to ring. My first job was out of town, and the premises were very grand, the reception area lavishly furnished.

"This is more like it," I thought! I was told to go round the back and that one of the lads would be there to open up for me.

Driving up to the mortuary door, I was greeted by a young man who helped me take in my equipment. Wow—what a Mortuary! Ten by four, a hand basin, and the body tray was a wooden door supported by two oil drums—and that was it! I'm sure I heard a voice in my ear saying, "Welcome to the real world of embalming, Jo!" The 'door' had been used regularly, so I knew it wasn't some kind of sick joke. Two happy souls brought a body in from an estate car and placed it on the door! I felt sorry for them, for I knew it wasn't their fault—they were just casual workers making a few bob.

I began to set up my stall, so to speak, and prepare the body. As I've said, I have to find an artery to send my formaldehyde around the body, and also a vein to drain out the blood. Everything was going well, but then I saw the bottle receiving the blood was getting full. I had to pour it down the sluice, but then discovered there wasn't one! I pondered, then looked at the tiny hand basin in the corner! No, I couldn't—and I wouldn't—pour it down there! Peeping out of the door into the yard, I saw a jolly soul cleaning a car. I beckoned him over and asked where one disposed of body fluids.

"No problem," came the bright reply. He told me to remove my protective clothing and make sure there was no member of the public in reception, and then quickly get to the loo and flush it down! (Was this guy for real!) With that he walked back to his shammy. So I had no choice but to check that the coast was clear and do the deed. I also poured a full bottle of bleach down and around the rim. Needless to say I wasn't at all happy.

Waiting for Work

On the way back from the 'ten by four' I had decided I wouldn't go there again, but the trouble with the embalming trade is that you never know what you're going into, and until you become established, you're not in a position to pick and choose.

Another job came up, and this time the mortuary was well equipped and spacious. But they only embalmed when 'necessary' and the body I had to do was going out of the country.

Whilst bringing in my equipment I noticed a large man leaning over a coffin, obviously attending to a corpse. I asked him politely where I could change and without looking up he pointed to a door that led into the staff toilet. I reappeared dressed in my garb.

The large man took one look at me and said, "Well, if it isn't Doctor Kildare!" Ignoring the fat bastard I started my work. I needed some suture and he was using some, so I approached him. As I reached him I could see what he was doing. He was packing the mouth of a corpse that had obviously 'gone off'. I commented on the state of the corpse, only to be told, "We don't do much embalming here"—and he proceeded to suture the mouth of the corpse.

"She's not being viewed, is she?" I asked.

"She'll be ho reet—she goin' tamarra," he replied coolly.

You dirty fat bastard, I thought. Not only was he using instruments on a decaying body, he was boasting that he didn't embalm much.

I was finishing off and the fat man came over, taking a look at the corpse I had embalmed. "He's goin' abroad or tha wouldna bin here," he said. Big fat stinking slug! I asked who paid me, and he put his hand in his pocket and pulled out a wad of notes and peeled off my fee. I couldn't believe it—*he* was the owner of that godforsaken place! I was never sent for again. I was glad, for that fat bastard was a health hazard.

I must say that all mortuaries are not like the ones I've described. The majority are very well run by caring staff, but there will always be a minority that have complete disregard for the dead; they will appear caring and sincere on the surface, but unless you can get behind their doors you'll never know, and maybe what you don't know won't harm you. Dead men tell no tales—but *I* do!

After some time I was offered a permanent position. Good, I thought, things were on the 'up'. The mortuary was old fashioned but well equipped, and I was given my own key. I was given a free hand to arrange everything the way I wanted. I was happy, at last, and set to.

A month passed and I was working steadily in 'my' mortuary. I was using up some of their embalming fluids but everything else belonged to me. Pay day came around and the manager said he had deducted some money from my pay package for use of fluids! I told him the chemical had been there for a while and that I was just using it up. He just shrugged his shoulders and walked out.

I cleaned up and started putting my 'stuff' in the boot of my car and then went into the office with the key, handing it to him. He looked surprised, but I left him nothing short. I told him I had pulled my 'tripe' out, had got the mortuary in shape and that we had a deal, and that no one pulled a stroke like that on me and got away with it—and that was the end of that!

My Friend Allison

I was feeling down and I needed a break. I had put my heart and soul into my work, I was completely dedicated, and yet I was meeting people that just didn't 'give a dam'! Nevertheless, they wouldn't change the way I felt about the career I had chosen. I was hooked on embalming and I was going to do it my way!

I set off to see my long-standing friend, Allison. She was an embalmer and also a FD, and always busy. I would turn up at her premises unannounced and help out. She had a serious nature and knew the business inside out. She was an excellent embalmer, too.

Allison was in the canteen when I arrived and, as always, glad to see me. We had a natter and she filled me in on the latest gossip. "Do you need a lift?" I asked, knowing what her answer would be.

We both went down to her mortuary. It was small, clean, and tidy. She was a stickler for cleanliness. I held open the fridge door whilst she grasped the body tray. She had said that the body had been brought in the previous night and so wasn't aware of its condition.

"My God!" Allison cried out. The tray was half in and half out of the fridge. I couldn't see much but noticed the body was a small elderly male that had part of his leg amputated. Then I saw it. What I *thought* was a leg stump was in fact his penis! I'm not surprised she'd exclaimed at the sight of it. My God, it was 'big' and yet the body was so tiny—but this only emphasised the pronounced size of the private part of his anatomy!

We carried on and treated the old man without any further reference to what we had seen. Allison was like me, dedicated to caring for the dead and compassionate when dealing with families.

Allison had to go out to arrange a funeral and asked me to finish off for her. I dressed the old man and was about to leave when Joe came rushing through the door. He was Allison's boss and needed a lift on a removal. Rather demanding of his staff, he looked put out that Allison had left, and said to me. "You can come with me."

"But I've never been out on a removal," I protested.

My words fell on deaf ears, and the next thing I knew we were in the private ambulance speeding off.

"I'm not dressed for this, Joe," I said. I was wearing denim jeans and sweater.

"Just do as I tell you when we get there," he replied.

Arriving at a block of flats, I was told by Joe to wait till he came back for me and the stretcher. I was beginning to feel a bit like a body snatcher! I also recalled the red haired apprentice when we carried out the stretcher and I was at the front end! As we reached the flat the warden held open the door for me and, without any further ado, I hot-footed it along the corridor to the bedroom, dragging Joe after me. I did feel some resistance from his end, but I kept going—and found myself staring at an empty bed. I turned to Joe with a puzzled look on my face which was beginning to turn scarlet. Then I heard a quiet voice saying, "She's in here."

She was in the bathroom where she had collapsed and died—an elderly lady dressed in a frock and pinafore. Lisle stockings came up over her knees held up with frayed elastic bands. I felt so sorry for the old girl.

On the way back I sat in silence. Joe said, "Ya know, Jo, not everyone dies in bed." And with a smile he thanked me and gave me twenty quid.

More Jobs Coming In

I was getting more jobs now that the funeral services knew I was available, and once again I was given the key to a mortuary not far from were I lived. I was able to go in at night, which suited me—I preferred working at night for then I didn't get 'called away.'

It was one winter's night when I had to go and embalm a case that was in a pretty bad state, having been dead a while. There was some facial damage I had to reconstruct.

Eventually I finished. It was getting cold. The little heater wasn't the best and it had taken longer than anticipated. But I only had to put the body in the fridge and I would be out of there. I began to wheel the tray towards the fridge when the lights went out! I knew where the other switch was at the side of the fridge—it would light up the coffin shop and enable me to see. I had been told about the faulty mortuary light.

Christ, it was dark! Nevertheless, I made my way slowly towards the fridge. Once there I reached over to hit the switch—but where was it? Running my hand up and down the wall, I leant further over and then heard something that chilled me to my bones! It was a rustling sound and my mind began to run riot! I had visions of a corpse walking towards me in a hospital paper shroud. Cursing myself, I tried again for the switch. The rustling just got louder!

I thought, should I shout out? But I couldn't—my heart was in my mouth! With one last attempt to locate the switch, I managed and the lights flickered on. I looked down and saw the cause of the rustling noise. It was my plastic pinafore against an incinerator bin at the side of the fridge! What a relief! Nevertheless, I had been shaken—there was no doubt about that. And another thing—I no longer felt cold!

I began to have nightmares after that night. One was so bad that I slept with the light on all night. I had done that before at Edna's! In my dream I was standing at the bottom of a flight of stairs looking up and saw a young woman descending towards me. She was wearing a long white gown and mouthing to me, her arms outstretched. I was telling her that I couldn't hear what she was trying to tell me. I thought she wanted to put her arms round me so I began to move back till I could go no further. She came within inches from me and lifted her gown to her waist, revealing bloody flesh and intestines, hanging from which were varieties of embalming instruments. She began to scream at me to remove them, but I was too busy screaming with her to do anything!

I had a couple more nightmares, but then they stopped—the ones you have in bed, I mean!

Flesh Eating Bug

I had been asked to embalm a lady that was going to repose at home. This called for the highest standard of embalming, for once the deceased is home you can't go knocking on the door to check the body. The staff placed the corpse onto the table whilst I was getting changed, and I heard one of them remark that one of her legs had been removed and I got a whiff of a very unpleasant smell.

On examining the body I saw that the right leg had been separated from the torso, looking as though it had rotted off! Dangling from a hole where her pelvis used to be was a length of intestine resembling an elephant's trunk. Large holes in her thighs were green and smelly. Her face was discoloured and skin torn on her poor hands, but the worst thing for me was that this woman had come from a hospital! No attempt had been made to dress the gaping holes. I was shocked and saddened by the way they had sent her to me.

I stood for a while trying to decide the best way of treating her. It wasn't going to be easy and I had to think on my feet. Fortunately she was going to be dressed in a gown, so I set to embalming her head. Both carotid arteries in the neck took my fluid round well. Next, her hands; using a vessel in each arm, I injected down and her hands cleared nicely. The same was done to the legs.

I had to treat the holes by injecting a strong fluid around each and then packing them with another chemical. The torn skin on her hands I repaired, and having relieved the body of most of its blood, I injected a strong chemical inside. After wrapping her up with wadding to waist level and washing her face and hair, she looked so much better. I had done my best so that she could rest at home with her family who, I might add, were very pleased.

I found out a few months later that the woman with the gaping holes had died from the flesh-eating bug! I was livid. I sent shock waves to the hospital where she had come from, but nothing came of it. I'm sorry to say that we embalmers as yet have no legal right to know the cause of death, but now there is a guide as to which cases are not to be embalmed. Not surprisingly, they've added 'The flesh eating bug' to the list!

A Quiet Time in the Trade

The funeral business can be quiet at certain times of the year, and I was beginning to wonder when my phone would start ringing again. It did, but I wasn't prepared for the case that I had to embalm.

Death has no respect for age. I was going to embalm a six year old girl, and I wasn't looking forward to it at all. Arriving at the funeral service, I asked for as much information as I could. (I had learnt my lesson well since the run in I had with 'The Hospital'.) Dealing with children demands a lot of skill and care from the embalmer. It breaks my heart to see dead children, but I have to be strong for the sake of their families and do what I have to do.

Everything ready, I opened the fridge door and saw the back of her head, dark curls spilled over the headrest onto the cold metal tray. I hated to see her there, such a little body, flanked by two adult corpses. Christ, why couldn't there be a special little fridge for small children and babies, I thought. There was no weight in the frail body I carried into the mortuary. I laid her on the table. She had been poorly for some time but had recently been well enough to attend her sister's wedding, and she was to be buried in her bridesmaid's dress.

With a heavy heart I prepared this child for her family. She looked lovely, as if in sleep; her once pale cheeks had taken on a warm glow and her dark curls caressed her face.

It was done, and I monitored a member of staff to bring in the clothes I would dress her in. The bridesmaid's dress was pink with tiny white roses embroidered around the collar and hem. I took in my hand the tiny white gloves. Completing the outfit were little white satin slippers. I was choked. My vision blurred and I set to and dressed her. One of the staff took her from me, and tears rolled down my cheeks as big as marrow peas.

I left her and drove home, feeling down. I felt another break was needed. I had just one more body to do and then I was going to chill out for a while.

I arrived early at the funeral service and was told the body was ready for me. The mortuary was tidy but antiquated, and once again no sluice. I asked where I should pour the body fluid, and was shown a grid in the alleyway outside. Oh Christ, this was too much! Fluid down, full bottle of bleach to follow, and I crossed those dirty bastards off my list!

My Cousin Linda

I needed another break, and what better than to pay my cousin Linda a visit!

Before Linda married we did everything together, but I wasn't too keen on her husband and only tolerated him for her benefit. I rang her and asked if it was okay to come over. I had picked a good time because her husband was away on some kind of course.

I arrived just before lunch and Linda hurried down the drive to meet me. Hugging me, she quickly led me into the dining room and began telling me about one of her neighbours who had taken her little boy Peter out in his push-chair. Both were involved in a road accident: a car had hit the pushchair, snatching it from the mother's hands. The child of two years was killed outright, the mother shocked but unharmed.

Linda had just been over to see him. "He's in a casket on the dresser under the front room window," Linda said quietly. "His mother is in a terrible state, Jo. She keeps coming for me to go and sit with him."

We had just finished our cuppa when Joan knocked on the door. "What did I tell you?" Linda whispered.

Linda showed Joan in and introduced me to her. The poor woman's eyes were swollen and red. She was under some sort of medication. Not taking much notice of me, she sat down by Linda and asked if she would go over; then she looked at me and said, "You come too," adding: "Do you know about my baby?"

She wasn't looking at either of us now, just gazing across at her front window. Linda took the woman's hand and said, "Come on Joan, we'll go over."

It was so sad. Peter's mother beckoned me to go over to the little casket, then took my hand and whimpered, "Don't be afraid." Stroking his brow and then picking up his hand, she told me to touch him. I did, but he didn't look good; his lips were blue and parted, as if about to make a sound that had been frozen on impact. He was a ghastly looking grey, but I was looking at this child through the eyes of an embalmer. Joan was looking through the eyes of a mother. She thought her baby looked beautiful and that is all that mattered.

Linda and I stayed for a while with Joan who wanted to talk about her baby. Then another neighbour came over with some flowers and we took our leave.

Joan didn't come back again. Later Linda told me the funeral was very tearful but that she had seen Joan since who was feeling a little better.

I told Linda that I would be over nearer Christmas to exchange presents. I had bought her a gold fairy on a chain. She collected fairies.

Linda is Poorly

It was getting near Christmas and I was preparing to deliver my cards and visit Linda.

The last time I saw her was when baby Peter had died, and I was looking forward to seeing her again and excited about exchanging presents.

All the house lights were on when I arrived, but no sign of Linda. I knocked on the door and waited. No one came, so I knocked louder and, peering through the glass door, I saw a figure slowly descending the stairs. It was Linda. She opened the door and could barely stand.

"What's wrong?" I asked in a concerned voice.

"It's my back, Jo," she groaned. "I've been in agony."

She looked awful and had dropped a serious amount of weight. I helped her into the living room and onto the settee. She put the back pain down to line dancing, but she looked very poorly to me.

I made us both a cup of tea and stayed until her husband came home from work. Then she said she wanted to go back to bed, so between her husband and I we got her upstairs, where we exchanged presents. I told her I would be back in a couple of days, and that I would bring Dave.

It was a Saturday night when we went over to see Linda. Dave took her husband for a pint—he looked like he needed one—and I sat on Linda's bed. I knew it was the end of the road for her. Now on stronger medication, she told me the pain wasn't as bad. Her doctor had said her back problem was through wear and tear. Well, he would, wouldn't he, being a first rate quack!

I asked her if she had sneaked a peek at the present I had bought her, and she smiled. "No, love," she said, "I'll wait till Christmas day." She wanted to sing some songs with me, so we started with 'Carolina Moon' and finished with 'Picture of You.' She sang and harmonised with me all the way through.

The next day she was dead. The Post Mortem revealed she had died from Carcinomatosis. In other words, Linda was riddled with cancer.

I was saddened beyond belief at her death. I was not asked to embalm her, but I knew the funeral service that was making the arrangements, and I went to see her.

God! What had they done to her! She was yellow! Dressed in a bright pink gown, hair swept back from her forehead under a mop cap, she looked ninety. Linda had beautiful hands but now they were thin and grey. Her sunken eyes told me that very little had been done for her. She looked so weary and cold. How I wish I could have cared for her, but it wasn't to be.

I laid a single red rose between her hands and straightened the gold fairy on the chain around her neck and whispered, "Sleep in Heavenly peace."

I made my way home thinking about that funeral service. I should have done it, I kept telling myself, but it was easy to say that now it was too late.

Linda's Death gave me more food for thought. What would *I* do if anything happened to my immediate family?

My Little Mother

My sister Jenny, whom I refer to as 'my little mother', had been having health problems and we were afraid it may be her heart. She was fifty-six when she suffered a major stroke, then became epileptic. Samantha and me cared for her like she was made of china. My mother had died, so we were all she had.

Being very independent, Jenny lived on her own; but I would visit often and we would take turns in having her over to stay, and she was always with me in times past, in whatever new challenge I faced. Jenny never complained about anything, and she was always encouraging me to go further with whatever I decided to do.

Jenny was staying with Samantha when she started experiencing breathing difficulties. I took her to the hospital where they kept her in for observation. They couldn't find out what was making her breathless. I was afraid it was her heart. I kept going up to see her and asking if they had any results, but I wasn't prepared for what they had to tell me.

I was taken into a side room and told by the doctor that Jenny had lung cancer! I was speechless. I couldn't go to her ward. She would know something was terribly wrong. The doctor said he was going to tell her, and I begged him not to. But it was no use. I sobbed at him: "She's been through so much—please, please don't do it,"—but the answer was the same: he was legally bound to tell her. "Well then," I croaked, "at least can you do it with her son present?" He agreed.

I walked out of that hospital numb from head to toe. I couldn't even turn the ignition key. I knew my Little Mother was dying! Her son confirmed it. She had about five months to live.

Jenny took the news of her cancer as a matter of fact. She had the courage of a lion, but I was struggling to stand toe to toe with it. I told my doctor I felt I was dying with her and he prescribed some medication to help me cope.

Once out of hospital we put Jenny in a private nursing home. The staff were so good to her and Samantha even got a job there to be on hand. I would bring her over to our house and push her out in her wheelchair, and day by day I could see my little mother fading away. I kept dropping my happy pills and would look forward to the rain, for when it rained she couldn't see the tears on my cheeks.

Jenny had always made it clear she didn't want anyone to see her 'in her coffin' and most definitely did not want embalming.

I often wonder if she was letting me off the hook, but could I have done it? I will never know.

Jenny's Death

Samantha and I decided to arrange for Jenny to go into a Hospice. Although she wasn't in constant pain, she was looking weary, and I was afraid the pain would come. But there was no need. She died the day before she was due to go in.

It was a Saturday afternoon when I went to visit her. The doctor had been the night before and given her an injection to ease a pain in her leg. She was telling me about it and asked me to massage the leg that had been giving her the pain. I used to do it for her when she had cramp. Samantha came in and Jenny told her I had massaged her leg and she felt fine, which is what she always said when I asked her how she was.

My Little Mother looked weary and I told her to try and get some sleep. I settled her down and left. I had not been home long when I received a call from Samantha asking me to go back—but "not to rush." When I arrived Jenny had 'gone'.

"Jesus, Jesus, Jesus," I cried when I saw her. Cradling her in my arms, I cried out to her how much I loved her, holding her so tight I could feel the warmth of her body. It seemed to soothe my anguish. Then I thanked the Father for taking her before the pain came back.

I was composed now and asked for a member of staff to help me lay my Little Mother out. We changed her nightie and washed her. Then I attended to her face and hair. I can honestly say that the weariness had left her, and after applying a little make-up and styling her hair, she really did look at peace.

I wanted to take her back to a friend's funeral home, but Samantha reminded me of Jenny's wishes, so I had to respect them.

They came to take my Little Mother away. Two men brought in a stretcher and placed it on the floor beside the bed. One of the men moved towards the door and half gestured me out. I told them who I was and that they could carry on. I also reminded them that she was very precious to me, and that I would be coming to see her, though I never did.

I have to say that the funeral profession does not in any way prepare us for death. We do not become hardened to it by seeing it all the time. It can be harrowing dealing with strangers, so what can we expect when death takes one of our own?

I wanted now to find out what it was like dealing with those that had been bereaved, so I took a job as a part-time funeral arranger. I wouldn't have to go out on removals so that was fine by me.

I was to be taught by a young woman called Jackie. She had run the branch for a number of years and what she didn't know about funerals wasn't worth knowing. She told me she was glad of my company. Being a small branch meant that at times one could get quite bored, and we got on like a house on fire. We would do mock arrangements and she would always play the part of a difficult client.

I came on in leaps and bounds and began arranging funerals on my own. Jackie had done me proud, and phoned me at home and said the little office was mine and wished me luck.

My Little Office

Loving every minute in 'my little office', I knew that if I needed any help Jackie would be there. I was looking forward to my next arrangement and I didn't have long to wait.

The phone call came from the mother of a three-year-old boy who had died of meningitis. This was going to be a tough one, I thought. I was in a different role from embalming behind closed doors. I would be coming face to face with the child's parents.

Both she and her husband arrived that afternoon. She was bearing up very well, and I wasn't convinced that it had hit her properly. Nevertheless, she knew what she wanted and I got on with it, the only problem being that our company did not allow the embalming of a meningitis case!

The mother asked me to let her know when they could 'see' their son, and I began to have doubts if they could. After they had left I rang the main branch and asked if they had the child? They had.

"What does he look like?" I asked.

"He's covered in a purple rash," came the reply.

Christ, I thought, but I went into my embalming mode and asked them to bring the child over along with some special chemicals. They arrived quick sharp.

I carried the little tot into one of the rest rooms and laid him on a table. I did not embalm this child but treated him externally with chemicals. The next morning I arrived to see that the 'purple rash' had faded significantly. I was then able to apply cosmetics to his face and hands.

I dressed him later that morning and rang his parents to come over. I had been advised to close the coffin the day before, but I could never deny anyone their goodbyes if there was the slightest chance that I could do something.

Both parents were happy that they were able to spend some time with their baby, but things may have been quite different had I not been there.

I was learning a lot about people's attitudes to grief. They all dealt with it differently. Some were in denial, others angry and some downright rude!

I never lost my cool but I came very close. I had a client in the office arranging her Aunt's funeral, and she was a pure 'Cow'! She reported me for being insensitive to her little boy. 'Little boy' indeed—he was a little swine! Whilst I was trying to go through the arrangements with his mother he made a B-line for my office and started to wreck it, pulling out plugs, throwing documents about and tearing up my tea bags, not to mention ransacking my drawers. He was a pure horror! I kept flashing my eyes in his direction but his mother never took hers from mine. She must have noticed the smile I was giving him wasn't a smile but a snarl!

I was glad to see the back of her and her little brat, and I was beginning to tire of funeral arranging. Reduced to vacuuming and dusting the rest rooms kindled my wanderlust. I was lonely and very bored, but I was saved from my boredom when asked to cover at a busy branch for someone who had gone off sick.

First Week of Cover

First week at the new branch was great and the administrator was no other than Jackie. The rest of the staff were great to get along with, too. There was never a dull moment in that office, the atmosphere always lightened by the odd joke or two.

Something happened there that will always make me smile at the memory, and it was no joke.

One of the FD's had been to the dry cleaners for his mourning suit and had left it in his car while finishing some shopping. On returning he found his car had been broken into, and amongst some of his belongings that were stolen was the mourning suit.

A few days later the same FD was to conduct a funeral. There was a large family gathering in reception to pay their last respects. It was time to go and the FD hurried them to the funeral cars, then went to close the coffin—and there was the body dressed in a suit, one that looked just like the stolen mourning suit. After checking the inside label, he stormed into the office, red faced and spluttered: "He's wearing my bloody suit!" I nearly fell from my chair.

My cover was nearly over and I was due back at my little office. It didn't appeal to me anymore, for I knew there was a distinct possibility that I could go stark crazy if I didn't change direction once again. I decided to be an embalming Tutor, like Fred.

I gave up the little office and only made myself available to embalm for holiday cover and sickness. I contacted Fred who gave me a telephone number of a teacher training college. I enrolled and had the option of staying there or using a hotel. I opted for a hotel.

Once there I met three others who wanted to become teachers—Phyllis, David, and Dan. We were given the rundown of the course which would consist of lectures and demonstrations of practical embalming. It sounded good to me, and there would also be a written exam after each session. It still sounded good.

I was looking forward to the next time, and we were told that before each weekend session we would receive a plan of what we had to do. I was chomping at the bit! Phyllis offered to pick me up on the way through. What a lovely gesture, I thought.

A letter arrived with an outlined plan for the coming weekend and I prepared my lecture and drawings. I called Phyllis to ask if she had got hers. She had, and was looking forward to seeing me again. I was happy at the thought that I had met someone with whom I could discuss embalming, since my Dave would hear nothing of it and had made it clear from the very start that he was only interested in the living and not the dead.

We chattered non-stop on the way. We were like two schoolgirls. I liked Phyllis, who was as keen as me to get on and had booked a room for both of us at the hotel near to the college.

First Training Weekend

This weekend would be the first of many and I was looking forward to getting started.

After our briefing we were to give our prepared lectures, and the training teachers would act as a 'class' of students. First up was David. He had been told to do about twenty minutes. He was very nervous and, I might add, very boring. In fact, one of the tutors asked if he would be much longer!

Phyllis was next and she went on and on for what seemed like twenty days! Again, she was very nervous—and then it was my turn.

I had been up in front of an audience many times, of course, so this girl had no nerves! When I had finished I went back to my seat, and someone asked where Dan was. In fact, he hadn't turned up. We all went across the road to the pub for lunch, and one visiting teacher leaned over to me and said, "Jo, you'll make a brilliant teacher." I thanked him, not knowing then that he was to become one of my dearest friends.

Lunch over, we made our way back to watch an embalming demonstration which was meant to prepare us for dealing with students. There were two bodies. One was 'straight', the other a PM.

In the huge mortuary we were told to gather round the body of our choice. I went to the PM. Whilst the tutor was going through the procedure, in walked a woman in a summer dress. She put on a pair of gloves and began to assist the Tutor.

I couldn't believe what I was seeing! She began looking for vessels, and her bare forearm was coming close to the corpse's ribs and no one said a word. I walked away and made my way over to the other case where a tutor was demonstrating finding and raising the carotid artery in the neck. He ruptured the jugular vein in his attempt and what a mess he made! There was blood all over and everybody laughed. He grinned and said, "This is what we call free drainage!" I wasn't laughing, though. Going through my mind was what a f—g sham it was!

We all left the mortuary and Phyllis and I went back to our hotel. We studied together and tested each other for the next day's session. There was still no sign of Dan.

Once again we gave our lectures and did a written test, after which we were taken individually to get our marks. I was called in and confronted by an elderly lady called Pam—rather plump—who spoke with a plum in her mouth. She told me that my marks weren't very high, but not to worry as it was early days. We then went for lunch, and who should walk into the pub but Dan! Pam rose to her feet and embraced him, saying playfully, "You're a little late, aren't you, dear?" Dan laughed and made some excuse, and sat close to her. Well not *that* close—he was a fat bastard.

Brian, one of the tutors I came to name 'Loose head', informed us that we would have to embalm a body that afternoon and that none of us would have any idea what we would get.

On entering the mortuary there were three bodies, each covered by a sheet. Why weren't there four? We were told to take our pick.

I'm the Underdog!

Mine was a straight case, as was David's; but Phyllis had got a PM case—and *he* looked awful! We were told to start and I could see no problems ahead of me. I noticed, however, that David had ruptured the jugular vein and looked as if he were mopping up the deck of a ship!

I was going steady in my own little corner and then I heard it—the voice of the 'plum mouth': "What strength of fluid are you using?" She must have had a bigger plum in her mouth than usual because it prevented her from smiling. I told her and she snapped back: "Convert into litres!" I replied politely that where I came from we used measures in pints and ounces. I was red faced, and she asked who my teacher was. When I mentioned Fred's name she just gave a loud 'tut' and walked away.

We finished our tasks and I took a look at Phyllis's case and it didn't look any different than before! Earlier I had noticed her being helped by Pam and Brian.

Brian said he would give us our reports, and then we would have a beer before getting back on the road. Good idea, I thought.

Back in the pub I brought my drink from the bar and sat down opposite plum mouth, who delved into her pocket for a piece of paper. "Could you read that to me, Jo?" The smile had returned. She must have changed plums when I wasn't looking.

Written on the paper was a poem in Lancashire dialect, and I read it through for her. She laughed loudly, too loudly for my liking, and said it was like a foreign language to her.

I looked at my report over my drink, as did Phyllis and David. Mine read that I had poor knowledge of fluid strengths and that although I was a tidy worker, they feared I had not put enough fluid into the body. Neither Phyllis nor David said anything but both looked very pleased.

Three days later I rang the mortuary and asked about the body that I had embalmed. They told me "it was fine."

I wasn't happy, but determined to see it through; and I had found out that these people hated Fred because he was totally against the way they ran things. If your face didn't fit, you were up against it, and if you were from the North of England, they saw you as a country bumpkin.

I fitted the bill, it seemed, so I was the underdog!

Another Weekend

Another weekend, and lo and behold, who should make an appearance but Dan!

Now, Dan was a self opinionated 'fat boy'—and I mean fat, and soft. Pam threw her arms around him and he giggled like a schoolboy.

He was asked to give his lecture. It was embarrassing, to say the least; he spoke to us as though we were infants, showing us little cartoon drawings of the human body! Another bore, worse than David, and I nearly slipped into a coma.

When he had finished all but one clapped, and a posh voice at the back of the room shouted: "Well done, well done!" Again, the fat bastard started chuckling like a big, big, baby!

My turn next. I had worked hard on my presentation, having been asked to speak for half an hour. It was timed to the last second and it was going to be good! But I was cut short halfway through as they needed to break for lunch! My presentation was ruined and I felt hurt. These bastards are beginning to close rank, I thought, and I was right.

After lunch we came back to do another practical. We were four now, and Brian paired us off, me with David, and Phyllis with Dan. Now, if ever two people clashed, they did. I was okay with David and we set to embalming our body. Tuts and sighs were coming from the other side of the room, not from plum mouth, but from Phyllis!

Bodies embalmed, we made our way back to the classroom to get our results. We had straight A's, whereas the other two were told they had done a 'poor' job and had only achieved C's. Ho dear! Phyllis was in tears, blaming Dan for the poor effort, but I couldn't care less. Our training was nearing its end, and I wondered how the 'fat boy' was going to fare. I could count on one hand the number of times he had attended.

On the way home Phyllis told me that at the next session there would be a guy called Bob who had recently become a teacher and had opened an embalming school. He would be available to answer questions on how to get started. I was looking forward to seeing him.

Rotten Teeth

Once again we were back in the classroom and I was looking for Bob. Pam introduced him to us and I took an instant dislike! He was the most arrogant, intimidating man I had ever had the misfortune to meet. Phyllis, on the other hand, liked him 'a lot'! She got on with him like a house on fire, or I should say 'arse'. Phyllis was no beauty but I'm sure she could have done better. Bob had bad teeth and his breath stank. He would come over to me to go over something I was writing and when he spoke I wanted to throw up!

Rotten teeth came again the next weekend and Phyllis kept her distance, swotting with me in our hotel bedroom as she always did. Even when we went for a drink she kept close to me, hardly speaking to Bob. There had to be a reason and I was soon to find out. It was the last weekend and we had to sit a final written paper; if we passed, we would be halfway to becoming tutors, for there was also a final practical exam.

Phyllis had called me and said she couldn't pick me up and that Bob had arranged a hotel. No problem, as far as I was concerned. Arriving early, I settled myself in and waited for Phyllis. She arrived alone and I helped her in with her case.

"I'm on the ground floor," she whispered. "It's a no smoker. I can open the window to have a puff."

It was a double room and Phyllis ran the shower and told me she had done her practical exam and passed.

"Oh!" I said. "Can you do that?"

"Yeah," came the reply from behind the shower curtain.

After she showered she came out and started to dress. She was flitting about like a teenager on her first date! War paint on, she said we would go for a drink. The sexy little number she wore was certainly not for my benefit.

In the pub she was telling me about the exam when in walked Bob! She told him, too—as if he didn't know. Getting back to the hotel I asked if she would like to do some last minute swotting, but Phyllis was 'bushed' and needed her sleep. Bob followed me up the stairs—he had a room next to mine and I bade him goodnight. Not being able to sleep I took a bath and started going over some notes when I heard a door opening. My timing was perfect! I held my breath and waited, then opened my door and tiptoed to the staircase. I was just in time to see Bob, minus shoes, disappearing into Phyllis's room!

I was at the breakfast table for 8.00am. Through the window I saw them both walking up the drive. They had been for a stroll. I mentioned my splitting headache and that I hadn't slept well. Bob said he couldn't sleep either and that he had got up and gone back to the pub for a nightcap. *Ho yeah*, I thought, *in your stocking feet!*

Final Written Exam

We arrived at the college and took our allotted places and guess who handed out the papers and sat in with us so that there would be no cheating?

After the written paper, we each had to give a lecture on our chosen subject, and then the teachers chose one for us. I delivered mine in great style, to Brian, Bob, Pam and Jed (the one that said I would make a great teacher). Then it was time for lunch. I knew that when we returned to the classroom there would be one more examination—an oral exam. The panel would fire questions at each of us and hopefully we would give them the correct answers.

I was called in first. There were only three teachers, for Jed had left, and the questions started coming. Brian first, then Bob and finally Pam, threw all they had at me, and I must admit I was struggling; but I kept thinking about Rotten Teeth and Hot Arse and that wasn't helping. While I was trying desperately to answer a question, Brian for some bloody reason started shaking his head very slowly, as if he were afraid it might fall off! I was then told to go downstairs and send the next one up, which was Dan. While he was up there Phyllis asked how I had got on. "Okay—I did struggle on a couple of questions, but that was all."

It was David next, and then Phyllis. The next time we went up would be for the verdict.

Phyllis was first up and I could tell by the peals of laughter that she had passed. Then Dan, who came back down pretty quickly.

"I've failed," he said, and dropped his head into his hands.

I'm not f—king surprised you failed, I thought, *you were rarely here!*

Someone passed him a coffee—it wasn't me!

David was next and he, too, passed. Then it was me. I sat in front of them and Pam asked for my thoughts on how well I had done.

"I think I've done okay," came my reply, and I went on to say that I had put a lot of work in and would continue to do so.

"Not good enough," said Rotten Teeth, interrupting me.

I heard Loose Head in a kind of whisper telling me not to give up. He went on to say that they couldn't pass me this time. "Sorry, Jo," he said.

I couldn't speak. I could just hear *sorry, sorry, sorry*—it seemed to go on and on. I left the room, numb.

There they were—the three of them. I walked passed them and into the toilet. I was fighting with every bit of strength I had not to break down. God, I had worked so hard.

I couldn't stay in the loo all day so I walked back into the room. David took me in his arms and—did I cry! He said softly that he had only just passed and that I, too, would get it next time. I had to get out of there.

Heading for my car, my heart was breaking. I couldn't even see the ignition hole! Then Phyllis knocked on the window.

"Don't drive home just yet, Jo," she said. "Come back in."

I managed to croak that I would be all right, and with that I reversed my car and was gone.

It was a bad move. I wasn't thinking straight and couldn't focus on the road. Signs were beginning to merge into one big blur. I should have been heading North—good old North. I needed my husband so badly.

Squeaky Fan Belt

Tears were still flowing, but I was beginning to pull myself together. The motorway was not familiar to me. I had missed an important sign and instead of being on the M6 I was hurtling down the M1 and low on petrol! I had to get off the motorway, and then I saw a 'Services' sign—which wasn't the only thing I saw.

A car passed me followed closely by another which I recognised as Bob's! Phyllis was in the first with Bob in hot pursuit! I followed them into the service station and watched as they both stopped and Bob got out and got in beside Phyllis. It looked like he was eating her! I felt nothing, only the satisfaction of knowing that she gave that toe rag her arse to get through her exams. There was no doubt about it!

For now I would keep it to myself. I knew I had something on them and it would keep till the time was right to bring it out into the open.

I managed to get back on the right track, and once home told David everything. "Well, what are you going to do now?" he asked.

"Ring Fred," I replied.

Fred was very sympathetic and also revealed that they really did hate him. He had upset them many times, and it looked as if I was their whipping boy!

"You'll get it if you persevere," he said.

Poor Fred—he had been so good to me and I thanked him for his time.

I decided to go and do my practical exam before re-sitting my theory. My examiners were Loose Head and Rotten Teeth. How lucky can I get!

Before going into the mortuary, I pulled Rotten Teeth to one side and refreshed his memory about the 'Motorway' occurrence.

"Oh yeah," he said. "Phyllis's fan belt was squeaking and she was afraid of breaking down, so I followed her to the service station."

That wasn't the only thing that was squeaking, I thought. They failed me!

Lost Joy

I re-sat my theory exam and missed it again by one presentation. It hurt, but I was told by Pam that if I did another and it was good enough, I would get a pass—so that wasn't too bad. Some new students wanted me to have a meal with them, so I went along. Brian and Pam came with us and we all ended up at a Chinese restaurant. The crack was good and I enjoyed talking to the rookies.

We had finished our meal and having our drinks when who should walk up to our table but Dan. After hugs and kisses from Pam he came over to me and asked how I had got on. I told him I had just missed by one presentation, and he hugged me tight and wished me luck for the next time. Dan left after a chat with Brian.

Later on I asked Brian when Dan would be taking his exam.

"He passed," came the reply. "He sent me homework and I passed him."

I couldn't believe what I was hearing!

"And what about his practical?" I asked, dumbfounded.

"He got that too. Dan's a good embalmer."

A good embalmer! He was f—g useless and Brian knew it!

The fat pig must have bought it. There was no way he could have got it on his own steam.

Phoney Bastards, I thought! Loose Head said, "Don't give up, Jo." Well, I had no intention of doing so.

When I went back to do my re-sit they threw everything at me—but I got it! I wasn't asked to go for the usual celebratory drink, and no one wished me luck. I was left outside the building struggling with my flipchart board and case. I called home and told Dave I had passed, but I had lost the joy of it. And there was one more hurdle to cross.

A Practical Nightmare

I put in for my practical exam and the date came through. I had been practising my embalming skills with Fred and I was ready for anything, including my examiners which were Bob and an elderly guy called Frank.

A student had been arranged for me and I was to supervise how he embalmed. We were told to get ready and make our way to the mortuary where we would find a body on the slab.

The body was that of a little old lady weighing about eight stone. I told my student to proceed. I was asking him what type of chemical he would be using whilst Rotten Teeth and Frank were watching like two vultures! The student told me he was using four ounces of formaldehyde to four pints of water. I nodded and told him to carry on, but Frank stepped in and told me to convert to litres. I said I didn't work in litres and the student looked puzzled.

"Try," Frank said. Feeling uneasy I said I can't, and Rotten Teeth wrote something down.

The student needed a jar and I went to retrieve one from the sink. It had about two inches of congealed blood stuck to the bottom, and Frank handed me a lavatory brush!

This time I didn't see either of them writing anything down. (*I* did, though—in my head.)

Passing the jar to my student I tried to put him at ease and just casually said that it was cold. That's all I said. When after about three minutes formaldehyde fumes were beginning to hurt my eyes, my student said nothing and just carried on. I asked if the extractor fan had shut down, and Fred replied sarcastically: "Ya said you were cold."

What a thing to do with such a toxic chemical! But I made a note of it in my head!

I was going to stand toe to toe with these two hateful bastards and things were about to get worse!

The Spike!

My student was having difficulty getting fluid to go into the old lady's legs and whilst I was explaining the alternatives, Frank opened a case and took out a vicious looking instrument; it was a small trocar. (Trocars are hollow metal tubes of varying lengths; some have blunt ends, some have sharp ends and this one was very sharp.)

Frank filled one end with a chemical, and completely ignoring me said to my student, "This is what you do when you can't get fluid in 'that way'"—pointing to the artery tube in the leg. Frank stabbed the old lady's legs until they resembled a sieve, and the chemical was leaking out all over. I began to cough and splutter. I told him I didn't see the need for using such an instrument, and that it was leaking fluid! Rotten Teeth snapped: "It won't harm ya!" I started to mop up till the spiker had finished his dirty work. I was disgusted. Her legs were an awful mess! I instructed my student to dress the legs and to make sure there were no further leakages.

I was beaten and they knew it, but I wouldn't have a slanging match in a mortuary.

All finished, we dressed the body and put it in a coffin. I was deeply saddened by the attitude of these two so-called teachers to me, and the complete disregard that they had shown to the deceased; in fact, she had been treated like a piece of meat.

My student thanked me and left. Frank popped his head round the changing room door and said he would be in touch with my exam results. He needn't have bothered—I already knew!

Three weeks had passed and neither of them had been 'in touch', so I rang Bob. He told me I needed more practice, and went further to say that both he and Frank were concerned about my attitude! That did it! I snapped back at him and told him I had bigger concerns than him and his sidekick!

I received a letter stating the reasons for failing me.

And it hurt. The letter from Rotten Teeth read that I was seen putting dirty instruments in a drawer, and that I couldn't advise my student on the best way to treat the corpse's leg, and that I lacked the attitude to be a teacher. But there was no mention of the Spike! Or the Jar with the congealed blood cemented to the bottom! Neither was there mention of the extractor fans. But *my* letter to the powers that be said it all. I gave the two Lowlifes the benefit of both barrels. I had them now, and boy, did I know it! I also included the squeaky fan belt and Bob's walk about in his stocking feet!

I was angry, but this time there were no tears. I applied to take the exam again, but this time with two different examiners. My request was granted and I awaited the date and venue.

I'm a Teacher!

I was on my way to Cornwall to take my practical exam. One of the examiners was Jed. Would he still be in the same mind about me? I hoped and prayed he would be, for I was becoming weary of trying.

I arrived early as usual and Jed greeted me at the door. He told me to go into his office and wait for the other examiner and my 'student' who would be a young lady. Jed plonked a cup of coffee in my hand and we waited.

He doesn't remember, I thought. *Should I remind him who I was?* But I thought better of it. I had been whipped so many times that should I whimper now I would be whipped again. Then, in walked my student followed by Allen. The girl was called Barbara, who smiled at me—which put me at ease. It was a sad fact that I hadn't seen many smiles in the last few months.

In the mortuary I began supervising Barbara who was firing questions at me non-stop. Jed but on some background music and both he and Allen watched us both.

All finished, and I was calm. Barbara had been a little gem, and she was going to be a great embalmer. Jed was her teacher and he was renowned for being the best around.

Leaving the mortuary, Jed suggested we go for lunch. Allen, however, had another engagement and apologised to me for not staying. He shook my hand and wished me all the best and was gone. Once in the pub restaurant, Jed went to get the drinks. Barbara was still firing questions at me and I was feeling uneasy. I managed a watered down smile as Jed sat opposite us, and it seemed an age before he spoke.

"You really want this, don't you?" he asked in a quiet voice.

"Yes, I do," came my reply. Barbara had shuffled closer to my side and was looking intently at my face. *God, I wish she wouldn't do that!* I thought. Jed went on to say that he and Allen had watched how I had instructed and advised my student, and were very impressed. He was giving me an unconditional Pass.

My eyes filled up and Barbara threw her arms around me with the words, "You're a Teacher!" It was then the marrow fats began to roll, but this time it was with joy. Barbara flew to the bar and bought me a short! *Teacher, Teacher,* kept ringing in my head. I had become weary of being verbally beaten up. I thanked Jed from the bottom of my heart, and he proceeded to advise me on how to start teaching.

On the train home I rang Dave to tell him the good news. He was relieved as well as happy. I was pushing that train home! I wanted to pull the emergency cord and tell all the passengers that I was a Teacher of Embalming!

It was all behind me now—the humiliations and the tears of despair had gone. I began to think how much it had cost me in effort and, indeed, cash! I would have to start teaching, but I wasn't hungry for money, I was hungry for revenge, to show those who had stifled my efforts, to prove to them that I was as good as if not better than all of them.

'Little Thimble Fist'

Back home Dave and I went out to celebrate my success with a few friends, who were coming up with ideas on how I should start teaching. In the meantime, however, I had to carry on embalming freelance, and there was no shortage of bodies.

A three year old had died tragically while on holiday abroad. I learnt that she had tried to retrieve her dolly that had slipped out of her hand and into the swimming pool of the hotel. The child had knocked her head as she went under the water. There wasn't a sound to attract the attention of anyone on that quiet afternoon. She was soon missed but it was too late. Her parents were distraught, and I knew that this was going to be a testing and very sad time for me.

The funeral service rang to say the child was with them. I went over at once. She was in the mortuary on a tray, covered up to her neck with a blanket. Above the blanket was a little brown face and blonde wispy hair, little gold earrings. I took hold of her hand and whispered, "Hello, little thimble fist." There was little bruise at the side of her face. Oh, poor little beauty! I had visions of her precious little dolly slipping from her grasp. *Jesus, why didn't someone see her?*

Her parents were going through hell. The father was doing the arrangements, as the mother was too distraught to do anything. Every time the child's name was mentioned the father broke down. It was up to me, now, to attend to this baby as skilfully as possible. I had to get on with it even though it was harrowing. When I had finished there was no sign of the 'bruise' and she looked as if she were having a nap. It was hell for me dressing her in a little mauve dress, which had a little cloth shoulder bag of the same colour. With a heavy heart I rested her head on a pillow and put the final touches to her baby hair. Placing the bag under her hands, I patted them gently and left.

Suicides

I was having a run of suicide victims. These can be very challenging to the embalmer and call for the best of skills.

The lad was just twenty-four years old and homeless. He had put his neck on a railway track in an attempt to sever his head under a passing train. As in all sudden deaths, a PM had been performed. His head was just sutured loosely in place and I would have to remove it. We had some maintenance men in the building, so I locked the door. I didn't want anyone of them walking in on me—some are very nervous and always seem to be rushing to finish whatever they have to repair!

Removing the head, I took it to another tray and proceeded to embalm it. The arteries leading to his head took the fluid and the darkness of his face changed to warm flesh colour. There were only superficial marks on his face and I covered these with filler and wax.

I treated the rest of his body and then secured his head in place. He looked fine. I cut his hair and trimmed his beard. Now he looked no more than his twenty-four years. There was no evidence of the trauma he had suffered. He was dressed in his own clothes, but no one came to see him. I did, though, every day until the funeral.

The next suicide was an old man who had slit his wrists. Well, one of his wrists was slit; the other was so deep that his hand was nearly severed! He had told his wife he would have an early night and she stayed up watching telly.

Later she went up to the bathroom and there he was in a bath of blood! The poor woman was beside herself. She had no idea why he would wish to end his life. Three months later I embalmed her! She didn't get over losing her soul mate and just faded away.

This next case sticks in my mind. A young man had thrown himself from a building after a row with his wife, and he had made one holy mess of himself. Most of his bones were broken and he had extensive damage to one side of his face. I spent a long time filling in the wounds and attending to the broken bones, some of which had broken through his skin.

His wife came to see him, and as the receptionist was busy I showed her into the chapel. Christ, this woman got to me! I asked her if she would like me to go, but she was oblivious of me. Leaning over his coffin she began whispering loving words. Sobbing, she took his hand and kissed the palm. I was crying with her—what was wrong with me? I left her and went into the loo and threw some cold water over my face. Looking up into the mirror I told myself, "Jo, the job's getting to you!"

As for the widow, she sent a thank you card to the FD, thanking him for the way he had cared for her husband. It wasn't him though—it was me!

Teaching

People wanting to be embalmers were ringing me up non-stop. I really did need to find somewhere to teach when, out of the blue, Allison called to say that Joe would be pleased for me to use his premises, and she offered to help out. (What a star!)

I always asked prospective embalmers why they wished to do it. The most common reply was, "I really don't know; it's just something I have always wanted to do." Believe me, they make the best.

I had gut feelings about others and refused to take them on. It was a morbid curiosity that steered them to me. Others, again, thought that embalming was cotton wool and cosmetics. Come to think of it, I knew someone who once thought that too!

I taught those that I thought had the character, courage, and compassion to become good embalmers. They had to have all these qualities to walk in my footsteps.

I have been asked many times if I would do it all again. In all honesty I have to say that as far as becoming a teacher was concerned, what should have been one of the happiest times of my life was completely destroyed by those who tried to keep me down. Indeed, I rose above them, but they took the joy from me.

When asked if I would still have become an embalmer, I say that I have only one regret, and that is, I wish I'd done it sooner.

I am no longer a teacher but a Practical Embalming Advisor; but if what you have read has given you food for thought and you do have a sincere desire to embalm, then read on.

I will now change complexity to simplicity—in the art of embalming. Take note, however, that the following passages should be used only as a guide by those wishing to train as embalmers or those that are already practising the art.

PART TWO:

CARING FOR THE DEAD

Introduction

Welcome to 'caring for the dead.' I will take you into the world of modern embalming without any complexities; I will simplify the art so that you will understand what has to be done to give a more lifelike appearance to a 'dead body'. Some embalming textbooks can baffle the reader who may never have seen a corpse, let alone embalmed one. This book is not a textbook and should only be used for reference to those seriously thinking of learning the art and preparing to take practical tuition.

The Ancient Egyptians

The word 'embalming' makes one think of pyramids, and mummies. The methods used by the ancient Egyptians of 'preserving' the dead are a far cry from the way it is done today. It is a fact, however, that 'mummies' that have been exhumed have been preserved for centuries, thus enabling mortuary science to study the bodies that were mostly intact. This tells us that the Egyptians' methods must have been to a high standard. Let's look at their techniques and reasons why they embalmed.

Techniques

These were carried out according to the status of the deceased.

Royal status

If the corpse was of royal blood, then the following method would have been used:

The internal organs would have been removed and placed in 'natron' (sodium salt). The open trunk would have been dried and filled with spices, herbs and bitumen (tar), and then sewn up. The whole body would then be immersed in a natron solution and left for about forty days, after which they would dry and straighten the corpse. The body was then mummified by wrapping it in yards of linen bandages that were soaked in oils. Between each layer of bandage would be placed valuables; these and the bandages would be secured by applying 'gum Arabic' which had the effect of sealing the body from the effects of the atmosphere. The body would then be placed in a sarcophagus and taken to a tomb.

Lesser status

Now we come to the treatment of those of a lesser status. An incision would be made in the side of the trunk and corrosive chemicals would be placed through the incision which would dissolve the internal organs. The body would then be immersed in a salt solution for forty days, after which it would be dried and the incision stitched up. The body would then be returned to the family. Not all bodies embalmed by this technique were mummified.

Peasants

Bodies of peasants were usually soaked in natron or bitumen and mummified.

The reasons for the ancient Egyptians embalming were religious. They believed that the souls of the dead would pass into the 'circle of necessity' and stay there for thousands of years, after which time they would return to enter their body, enabling them to go and live with the gods in eternity.

Modern Embalming

Modern embalming is not practiced for religious reasons. We are not looking for permanent preservation, as were the ancient Egyptians. What we are looking to achieve is sanitation, preservation, and presentation. (Short term.)

We know that micro-organisms will cause a body to decompose, and although we cannot stop this process from happening we can retard it by the use of the embalming chemical 'formaldehyde'. The human body has a network of blood vessels that carry blood around it, and if we can replace the blood with formaldehyde, then we can saturate the tissues thus preserving the body.

Remember also that the human heart is a pump. We can also replace its action by using a 'mechanical' pump to send our preserving chemical around the body. How is this achieved? I will go through this later, but for now I need you to know about the chemical 'formaldehyde'. It's a water-soluble gas, heavier than air and very toxic. Extractor fans in mortuaries should be at knee level in order to extract any fumes that exude from the use of it. If this chemical is not used according to instructions it can cause irreparable damage to the upper respiratory tract. One must always wear protective clothing while using it. The mortuary is not a dangerous place as long as the embalmer follows the rules. Protect yourself first, for no harm can come to the 'body' on your table.

The Systems of the Body

One of the most important systems of the body is the circulatory system. It is by means of this system that we send the formaldehyde around to saturate and preserve. Unless you have studied this system you would be unable to embalm. The aorta is the largest artery in the human body, having lots of branches that feed the tissue. It is the vessel that will carry the embalming fluid around and distribute it to most of the tissues. Getting the fluid into the aorta is achieved by finding and raising one of its branches. For simplicity we will go through six. These are the carotid arteries, one at either side of the neck. The auxiliary arteries, one in each armpit. And the femoral arteries, in the groin of each leg. These are the main arteries that will carry the formaldehyde via the aorta around the body. I will explain in further detail later. You would also need knowledge of the 'Venus system' to be able to embalm satisfactorily. Remember that the arteries take blood away from the heart, whereas veins take blood to it. There is no need to worry about superficial veins to any degree. Each of the main arteries are accompanied by a main vein, and it is these that as an embalmer you should be interested in.

Total irrelevance

One of the most frustrating times I had when I was an embalming student was the total irrelevance to embalming in the text that I had to study. One had to know in depth about all the systems of the human body. I will take you through them and also dismiss some as sheer page-fillers that made the textbook look important enough to warrant payment from the student! Let us take the digestive system; there is no need for anyone other than a doctor or a nurse to know anything in depth about this system. And the only thing you need to know about it is that after death, the stomach can give up a brown fluid that can exude from the body's mouth, usually containing hydrochloric acid; it can burn the sides of the mouth and to prevent this the embalmer should aspirate the mouth, clean away any fluid and put massage cream around the lips and chin. This will stop the acid from burning. And that is it—to know any more is of no consequence, yet some embalming books go into great detail of what happens to a 'cheese sandwich' from the moment it enters the mouth until it is expelled via the back passage. Why? They're dead!

The respiratory system

Again, some embalming textbooks go into great depths as to the workings of the respiratory system, how oxygen is breathed in and utilized in the blood. Breathing oxygen is essential for us, but not for the deceased! The important thing for the embalmer to know is that the lungs can also exude a frothy fluid after death so one has to place an aspirator in the body's mouth to drain it off, and to keep it there whilst embalming. Who needs to know how many lobes the right lung has and how many the left lung has? And the structure of the alveoli—unless you're in the medical profession! The only thing the embalmer needs to know is where these systems are, by surface projection—something I will cover later.

The nervous system

Now, if ever a system was totally irrelevant to the embalmer, this is one. Why do we need to know about the autonomic nervous system? We don't. And as far as the three *meningees* (linings of the brain) are concerned, we only need to know about one, and that is the 'Dura mater'. This is a tough lining that can be seen in the skull cavity after a post mortem. It needs to be removed, as there are little veins beneath it that can leak, something that must be avoided; but as far as the other two are concerned, they are of no consequence to the embalmer—unless he is thinking of becoming a brain surgeon!

So we have looked at the three systems of the human body which contain organs, and which need to be treated with formaldehyde. If the body is a 'straight case' you will not be able to see the organs of these systems, unless you have learnt your anatomy. The embalmer can treat the whole body by surface projection; in other words, we need to be able to 'see' through to the areas that we need to treat. I suggest, therefore, that you buy a book on human anatomy and get studying. If the body has had a post mortem, then there will be no need to look for the internal organs, for they are usually in a plastic bag. All you'll have to do is pour some disinfectant over them. But you will still have to find the arteries in which to inject your formaldehyde. Don't worry, I will take you through it.

The Skin

Here we go again. 'The skin'—well, what about the skin? You do not need to know too much about it other than that it could be damaged either by trauma or the natural process of decay; in either case we must know how to deal with it.

The main thing is that parts of the body that will not be visible to the deceased's family can be treated and covered. The face and hands cannot. So, depending on the amount of damage, skin can be a problem, especially if it is on the 'face'. There are lots of mortuary waxes and cosmetics that can be used for damaged skin, but again there is a certain amount of skill involved and that cannot be learnt by just reading about it; one has to have a go, hands on, to perfect the oper-ation. And, indeed, the body has to be embalmed before it is restored. There is no use applying waxes and cosmetics to a decaying body!

Embalming is not hard, but a matter of knowing where the vessels are to inject your fluids, and knowing what kind of fluid to inject. There are many different types for special cases. As I have said earlier, in my opinion all embalmers should be qualified, but getting qualified is something else. I would say that if you found an embalmer with a good reputation who could teach you the practical side of embalming, then you would only have to tell the funeral service who you have studied with and, providing you were ready 'to go it alone', that would do. As yet you do not need a certificate to say you're qualified; if you're good enough you will always get work embalming.

Making a Start

Let us consider the health and safety of the prospective embalmer.

It is worth remembering that you're dealing with 'dead bodies', and although I have never heard of anyone dying from such an occupation it would be foolhardy not to be prepared for the vocation you've chosen. The first thing to do is to have a course of injections. Your doctor will give you the necessary shots; you should not work with the dead without them.

The next thing is your protective clothing. I was once referred to as 'Dr Kil-dare', but I still wear the appropriate garb. You need it, believe me. Whatever I tell you is for your safety. You will need the following:

a.   Surgical gloves

b.   Theatre gown

c.   White boots

d.   Goggles

e.   Long plastic pinafore

You will also need to be familiar with the machinery in the mortuary. This is best achieved by participating in a funeral service (not that easy) and asking if you could observe an embalming. Offer to 'help out for free'—as long as you can 'get in'. Don't write—knock on doors, as I did. If you're lucky enough to know a trade embalmer, ask to go out with him or her. Trade embalming can be a lonely existence; the person may welcome your company.

Okay? Right, then I will go through the mortuary machinery with you, just in case. Remember I told you about the circulatory system and the vessels that carry blood around the body? It's the heart that pumps the blood around in life. In death we replace this action mechanically.

Mortuary Equipment

The pump

The pump consists of a pressure gauge of varying levels. One must always start off on a low pressure to begin with and then build it up slowly; an ideal pressure is said to be 51bpsi, but in my experience the body dictates the pressure and the treatment by its condition. Leading from the pump are two tubes; on the end of the outlet tube is your artery tube, usually metal, while the other tube is used for aspirating fluid from the body.

The embalming table

This is usually metal—hydraulic to enable easy manoeuvrability of the body; however, I have embalmed on a wooden door!

Sluice

This is where one disposes of bodily fluids.

Incinerator bin

This is for soiled dressings.

Sharps bin

For sharp instruments.

Good mortuaries will have non-slip floors, no porous surfaces to attract bacteria, and good working conditions; but beware—there are mortuaries from hell!

Embalming fluids

There should be a variety of these for different body conditions.

Cosmetics

Your embalming kit

◆   ◆   ◆

A lot of students buy their equipment before they have even seen a dead body, let alone embalmed one—and there is no need. Most embalming books will give you a list so long that you will fall asleep before you get to the end, and instruments do not come cheap. Let's look at what I have in my embalming kit:

Instruments
2 Aneurysm hooks
2 pairs of scissors
1 set of vein tubes
1 set of Artery tubes
2 pairs of Dissecting Forceps
Set of Hypodermic needles
Set of Suture needles
Two separators
Set of Artery Clamps
Scalpels
Suture
Trocars
This will be sufficient to embalm a body.

Sundries

Cotton wool

16onz Bottles of different chemicals

Mortuary cosmetics

Shaving equipment

Manicuring set

Hair dryer

Shampoo Wet/Dry

Eye caps

Glues

Embalming Equipment

Pump (Electric)

Pump (Hand)

80onz Jars (2)

I bought all my equipment second hand. I advise the same for you.

Chemicals and their uses

You will need to understand the chemicals you are going to be using. For example, formaldehyde has to be injected into the body diluted. If you look at the label on a 25 litre container of formaldehyde you should find details about the type of chemical and the strength of the chemical. There are chemicals for 'problem cases' that have a marked degree of decomposition. The strength of gas in the solution could be from 25% to 30%. Embalmers are advised to use a working strength of between 1% and 2% so this chemical must be diluted to inject, and it can be done with ordinary tap water.

A special chemical is needed for jaundice cases. You may like to know that if you have a jaundiced body you should not use 'ordinary' embalming fluid; the colour of this fluid is usually pink, so once injected the body will turn from yellow to deep green. This is because the pink fluid will mix with the bile pigment in the blood (Bilrubin) and convert it to Biliverdin. ('Verdin', meaning green.) This staining of the skin cannot be removed, so what is the answer? Cosmetics and special chapel lighting. If you are aware of this, then why not have a 16onz jar of special jaundice fluid? Problem solved. A note of caution: jaundice is a sign, *not* an illness. You must find out what caused the yellow discoloration of the skin before embalming! It could be very infectious!

There are so many chemicals on the market and you would be advised to send for the fact sheets; these will tell you the dilutions and strengths to give the best results.

Cavity fluid

Cavity fluids must be used neat. They are not meant to be injected via the circulatory system. This chemical is usually applied by inserting a metal tube into the area to be treated. I will go through instrument use later.

Please note that embalming chemicals must never be mixed unless they are compatible.

There are also chemicals that can build emaciated tissues; one that is very pleasant to use can be mixed with embalming fluid and is excellent for bodies that have died from a wasting disease. There is a chemical for Oedema (Fluid in tissues) that will reduce the fluid build up.

There is something for anything; there is no limit to what you can achieve with the right materials and a little practice. In the embalming trade there are never two cases alike. You are constantly being challenged in the art. Perfect it and you will always be in demand; abuse it and you will be 'seen through' very quickly!

Finding Vessels in a Straight Case

As I told you earlier, finding a vessel to inject your embalming fluid will be beyond you if you have not studied anatomy. You do not need to take a degree in this, but it would help to see an embalmer raising the arteries as well as looking in anatomy books; you will be surprised at what you can learn from watching.

Let's look at the carotid arteries in the neck, one on either side; they are deep in the neck muscles for protection. An incision is made just above the clavicle (collar bone) close to where it joins the sternum (breast bone) on the right side of the neck. The incision should be no more than 3". You will not see anything, only tissue, so keep close to the trachea (wind pipe); the tissue must be broken into by gently using an Aneurysm Hook. The carotid artery is in a sheath accompanied by the jugular vein. If this is ruptured in the process, it will make one holy mess! A finger inserted in the incision towards the trachea should touch what feels like a large elastic band. That's it—the carotid artery.

It needs to be 'teased out' gently, with the hook, away from the jugular vein. Once out, you can secure it with suture so as not to lose it. Arteries have a habit of slipping back!

Once the carotid artery is 'up' and secured by loosely tying a piece of suture, hold the suture with a pair of artery clamps. Next, the vein. Remember I said that veins take blood to the heart, and we need to relieve the body of this blood and replace it with formaldehyde. What better way than to 'tease' out the jugular vein next to the carotid artery. It needs to be done with great care, but once you have learnt to recognize it, you will want to use no other. Both artery and vein are nearest to the heart, which should ensure good distribution and good drainage. Once the vein is up, a separator can be placed under it (a flat piece of metal/plastic about 4" in length); this will enable you to nick the vein with a scalpel blade, just enough to insert a tube long enough to enter the 'heart'. This tube must be tied into the vein and the other end of it must go into a container that will receive the blood.

Next is that artery that you secured. Remove the separator from under the vein and put it under the carotid. Nick the artery so that you can 'slip' the artery tube in, and tie it securely. Once you begin to inject embalming fluid into the carotid artery, by sheer pressure the blood will be forced out through the vein tube. Always remember to inject first towards the heart with any vessel that you choose, and always 'drain' from the heart.

I have to tell you, however, that some embalmers do not do venous drainage! They will try to get as much embalming fluid into the body, then by using a long hollow metal tube called a trocar they will pierce the heart and drain the blood from it. I can also say that you cannot tell after a body has been embalmed whether the embalmer did venous drainage or drained from the heart.

Let's just consider the merits of vein drainage. Some cases will have discoloured faces, but using the jugular to drain from should relieve this discoloration.

Then let's say you are not going to use it and drain from the heart. If there is a back-up of blood in the facial area as you're embalming, the face will begin to discolour even more and you will have to relieve the blood by piercing the heart; but if you pass through the heart and damage a major vessel, your embalming fluid will not be carried around to the tissue, and if you have to 'pierce' before enough fluid is in the body, then you will have to lift the other five vessels in order to embalm the body as a whole.

Confused? Like I said, go and have a look at this procedure. It is better to see 'hands on' than read about it, and it will stick in your mind, I promise you. You will become a good embalmer by watching it for real and not by reading about it.

Ask to see how vessels are 'lifted', and ask to see how to pierce the heart; you only need to see it done a few times and you will be able to have a try.

The Auxiliary Artery and Veins

These vessels are fine to use if the body is female. We must remember that there can be visible signs of where the incision has been made, and if 'she's' going to be dressed in, let's say her wedding gown, then best keep away from the neck.

To find the auxiliary artery and vein is to 'feel' for an indentation just below the armpit; it is here that you will make the same incision as with the 'neck'. There are more little branches in this area so you have to search for the artery; again, observing this being done by a 'good embalmer' will help you tremendously. The vein can easily be seen, and lifting these vessels is the same as with those in the neck. Remember to inject *towards* the heart and drain *from* the heart. Even in the arm you can insert a vein tube long enough to reach the heart. Remember to start at the right side of the body, i.e. right carotid, right axilla, right femoral. You can go over to the left if for some reason the chemical is blocked from reaching that area.

The Femoral Artery and Vein

These are found at the top half of the leg. Stand at the right side of the body and place your left thumb on the hip, fanning out your hand to lay on the pubic bone. Your index finger should be above the indentation, which is where both vessels are located. Ask to be shown; it does work same as before for lifting. Remember that you can inject the whole body from one injection site.

Remember to observe the body whilst it is being embalmed. Watch for areas not receiving the chemical, for these will need to be treated sooner or later.

Now let's get back to the carotid arteries in the neck of a straight case (not PM). From the right you have injected down towards the heart. The body has got plenty of fluid in its arms and legs—good. Do not use *all* your fluid. Check to see if the face needs some. If it does, then stop injecting and turn your artery tube towards the head, secure with clamp or suture and inject. Keep the pressure low. The face can easily be distorted by over embalming. You should see the eyes filling out. Have a look—don't let them swell up. Look at the lips—they should be a good colour, and check the ears to see if they are clear of any discoloration. Remember, too, that the right side of the face is taking more fluid than the left side. Go over and lift the left carotid artery, and level the features up—you can do it with a little practice. I can tell you that I have a student who was able to lift the carotid artery and vein after watching me several times; she did it on her own and the body was fine. You, too, can do it. Make sure, though, that the embalmer you are watching knows his stuff.

Now think back about what I told you about the nervous system. The brain itself will decompose very quickly and if the arteries that you are injecting fail to deliver the fluid to the brain, the body will go off big time! So how do you know if the brain has been embalmed? Look for signs. The body will indicate to you that something is not right. The face will not clear well and there may be a persistent flow of fluid from the nose. It's no good shoving loads of cotton wool up the nostrils to stem the flow. What needs to be done to stop this purge is to take a small trocar that will be long enough to reach the brain, through the nostrils; once the trocar pierces the brain, aspirate and then inject 'cavity fluid'. This is the chemical that is used neat. This will ensure that the brain is treated and the purge will stop.

As far as embalming goes, we must always follow the rules. Do not do anything to a body unless it is absolutely necessary. To be able to embalm without mutilation is the best way, but unfortunately this depends on the condition the body is in, and indeed the cause of death, and we must always treat the body with the utmost respect. I would not wish you to have visions of me lurking behind a mortuary door flashing my trocar like Zoro or wielding my scalpel like Scaramouche! It is worth keeping in mind that embalmers are not exempt from death; do unto others as you would have done to you.

The Arms

The vessel that is used for the arms can be the auxiliary artery. Once you have lifted it, you can then nick the vessel and secure your artery tube. You will inject towards the heart. You will see superficial veins rising with the pressure from your pump and if you have raised the vein as well, you will see the venous blood coming along the vein tube. You can then clamp off the vein tube for a time and then release it. The build up of venous blood will be pushed out by pressure build up. We need to remove as much venous blood as we can—we need all the room in the body for the embalming fluid.

Look around the body. Is everything getting the fluid? Is the body looking warmer? And are the features fuller? (Not too full.) Yes, but the right hand isn't getting anything! No problem. Turn the artery tube round and inject downwards towards the hand—it *should* go in; if not, you can inject with a hypodermic needle between the fingers to get the chemical in.

I have seen embalmers struggle to find tiny branches in which to inject the fluid when the main one is either missing or blocked. It is hard work on your own, but there is always the hypodermic needle that will do the job once you have been shown the best points to use it. Keep in mind, especially with the face, that if there is a tiny artery and you can reach it, try to inject fluid into it; if not, use the hypodermic. A point to keep in mind: arteries have three coats. Make sure the tube slips in easily. If it doesn't, you may be between coats. Your chemical won't go in, so try again.

The Legs

Once the artery is lifted, inject towards the heart. You should be able to see the arms and face receiving fluid and also the left leg. This is because the network of vessels in the body is carrying the chemical around to the tissues. Medical textbooks refer to it as 'collateral circulation'; it is a fact that where blood flows in life, embalming fluid will flow the same path in death. Then turn the artery tube towards the right foot. If no fluid can get down, then inject between the toes, but get it in! The foot will not embalm on its own.

(Once again I must remind you that this book is not a 'Teaching' book on embalming—it is a simplified journey on how to care for the dead that is acceptable both to you and the bereaved.)

Many other vessels can be lifted to inject a chemical and that choice would be down to you when you are good enough. For the time being the simple way would be sufficient to embalm a body without any problems. It is only when things begin to go wrong that the embalmer must be able to put it right. Whilst you are learning, never take on anything that is beyond you. I can promise you that practice *does* make perfect, so don't ever rush an embalming. At first you will be painfully slow, but your speed will come when you least expect it. You have only one crack at embalming a body; once it is in the chapel and the family is viewing, there must be no complaints from them.

The rest of the body

Once the injection process is over, there are other parts of the body that need 'treating' and, as this is the straight case, it will be the internal organs. This is done by inserting a trocar into the body. An incision is made approximately 2" from the right of the navel, then 2" up. A long trocar must be used, as you will need to enter the throat.

The trocar will drain any body fluids in the trunk cavity. It will also pierce the internal organs as you 'fan' around, draining any residue. The trocar must be pushed into the throat to clear it. Once satisfied that no more or very little fluid is draining out, you can withdraw the trocar, rinse and then do the same with the bottom half of the trunk. With practice you will be able to relieve the bladder of any urine, but you must not pierce the intestines. After this 'trocar work' is done you can then proceed to disinfect the internal organs with neat cavity fluid. Using the same trocar, attach it to a tube which feeds into a special bottle filled with cavity fluid; tip the bottle up and the chemical will run down the tube into the body. Make sure that you follow the path when you aspirated the residue with your trocar. This will disinfect the internal organs.

All incisions must now be packed, closed and sutured. All orifices must be packed. The features must be set, mouth closed. If it is a gentleman he may need a shave; if it is a lady she may need cosmetics. Look at the hands. Check the nails—are they clean? Dress the hair. Do they look warm and peaceful? Walk round the body. Ask yourself if you would be satisfied with what you have done. Only then can you leave if you want it to be right. I have stayed with bodies for hours till I have achieved what I wanted. If you want to be 'a quick squirt merchant', then embalming is not for you. I would say that an embalmer should try to put at least twelve pints of fluid into an adult body. A rough guide is 1onz of fluid to one stone in body weight. Some bodies will take more, others less, but if you can see that the body is 'embalmed' then you have put enough in.

Finding Vessels in a Post Mortem Case

Post mortems are carried out to establish the cause of death. The pathologist will have the brain removed as well as all the organs in the trunk so he can examine them, after which they will be put back in the trunk cavity, usually in a strong plastic bag. Once you have the body in your mortuary the embalming treatment is different than the straight case. First, the body needs to be washed with a disinfectant, and observed to determine which is the best chemical to inject. Next, there will be two incisions—one in the trunk and one in the scalp. The trunk is opened and the bag removed. Cavity fluid—about 30onz—is poured over the contents. There will be packing in the neck and packing in the pelvic basin, which needs to be removed. There will also be the sternum (breastbone); this is best put in a bag with a powder disinfectant. I always put a little disinfectant in the trunk and then gently pour on 'cold' water, which I then aspirate; this action takes away any smells and also disinfects the area. Next, the head; after removing the scalp sutures the top of the scalp is brought forward. The top of the skull will have been removed to take out the brain, which was in the plastic bag. In place of the brain will be wadding. This is removed. Now I have a skull cavity and the top of the skull. This can have the same treatment as the sternum. Remember the Dura mater? It must be removed. It looks like a deflated flesh coloured balloon.

Finding the vessels

After removing the Dura, the skull cavity is rinsed out. Now I need to look for those carotids. They are both intact. Slipping the artery tube into the right vessel I need to inject my chemical at a low pressure. At the same time I will look in the skull cavity for my injected fluid. What happens in a PM case is that because the brain has been removed, the little arteries that feed the brain are a continuation of the carotids. They 'don't know' that the brain has 'gone' and they are still supplying fluid to it; but this time it isn't blood, but formaldehyde; no use letting it flow away, so these little vessels must be clamped off—there are only two.

Now I need to look at the face of my subject. Is it changing? Is it looking like it is clearing from a death grey to a warm pink? Yes. I can't emphasize enough not to over-embalm the face. So long as it clears to a warm colour and the eyes fill out (sometimes the eyeball shrinks and sinks a little), and the lips look fuller, then everything is fine. Both carotids must be injected as a rule.

Arms

The arms can be injected from within the trunk wall. In a PM this vessel is called the 'Subclavian' and is located just under the cut end of the top rib. (Ribs are cut to remove the sternum.) Injecting towards the hand will saturate the whole limb. There is a left and a right.

Legs in a PM case

Injecting the legs: the arteries used in a PM case for the legs are the 'illacs'. These can be seen in the lower trunk. Both right and left can be injected towards each limb to conclude the embalming process.

Other parts

If any part of the body has not received fluid, hypodermic injections can be used. The next thing is to dry the trunk cavity and place wadding in the neck and pelvic areas. A good powdering of the trunk will ensure the disinfecting of it. Then the plastic bag with the organs in is put back into the trunk cavity; the sternum in its bag is placed on top; then the trunk incision is sutured. I will once again wash out the skull cavity and dry it. A piece of cotton wool should be placed in the hole in the skull where the spinal cord was. Then wadding the size of a brain is put into the skull cavity. The top of the skull is put back and the scalp is sutured to hold the top of the skull in place. The features will now be set—nose packed and mouth sutured if it needs suturing. Sometimes in PM cases the wadding that is put in the neck will hold the mouth closed, thus eliminating the need for suturing. The most important thing about embalming PM's is that there are no leakages. Check the body for any puncture marks caused by canulas that may have been used in the hospital. Look closely at the hands and ears—make sure there is no blood around, as can often happen with these cases.

Embalming children

Embalming a child is the most delicate operation you will ever have to do, aside from the emotional aspect of such an undertaking. Forget 'adult' embalming for now. Most children have been the subjects of a PM, but finding the tiny vessels is like finding a needle in a haystack. Don't let this worry you. Let's look first of all at a child PM. The organs will be in a plastic bag, so these can be treated with cavity fluid and put to one side. Next, the tiny trunk cavity can be 'treated' either by an embalming gel that is smeared all over or an embalming powder. The skull is very soft but it must be treated the same way as any PM. Let's say that the case is approximately two years of age. We do not suture the mouths of babies. The face can be treated by injecting from inside the head. There are also 'soft' embalming chemicals that can be used on tiny faces. In fact, a child that has had a PM is easier to embalm than a child that hasn't. I will take you through the requirements for children.

Still born

These babies will have a sterile gut, so decomposition is slow. Make sure that the face is clear by use of soft embalming chemicals. Mother may wish to hold.

0 to 1 years

Skill needed to locate aorta. Incision made below umbilicus. Liver is large in babies—need to go to the right, close to the middle of the body. Locate aorta and inferior Vena Cava (vein that runs alongside of aorta). Rare, but I have had babies this young that have not had a PM.

1 to 5 years

The femoral artery is usually the best, as children of this age have short necks. Try not to make things difficult for yourself—go for the femoral artery.

5+

The carotid artery or the femoral can be used.

A word of caution

Make sure you have gained either the knowledge to undertake the embalming of a child or that you are under expert supervision. There is nothing like hands on experience to give you confidence, and when it comes to children you will need it.

Regarding the kind of embalming chemicals for children, there are special fluids that you can buy. Embalming suppliers are happy to assist in the choice. However, one quarter of the strength of embalming fluid is the norm for small children. If the strength is too high, it will most certainly burn the tiny vessels that are meant to carry it around. Ask what is the best type of fluid for children; new products are coming out on a regular basis.

Special Techniques

There are conditions of the body that require special techniques. The condition of a body can be so bad that it is beyond the normal embalming operation, but that does not mean 'no' treatment is possible. If a body cannot be seen, it will obviously need to be sealed; indeed, there are bodies that are infectious and must not be embalmed. (You can get a list of these diseases.) They will be in 'body bags', but the bag will not prevent the body from decaying and giving off odours. The best thing to do is place the body in its coffin that has been lined with wadding soaked in cavity fluid; then lay wadding over the top—again, wadding that has been soaked in cavity fluid. Cover immediately with a plastic sheet. The fumes from the cavity chemical will 'get to you' if you dilly-dally. The plastic will help prevent this, and then close the coffin up. Visiting family and friends will be able to 'sit' in with the coffin, and it is important that they can do this without any unpleasant odours coming from it.

Drowned bodies

A person who has drowned will need treating with a strong embalming solution. Bodies that have been in water even for a short time will begin to decompose very quickly, especially the face, which will have been in contact with the water. Unfortunately, restoration of the face may be impossible, but every effort must be made before deciding to 'close the coffin'.

Burnt or scalded skin

Depending on the degree of the burnt skin and indeed where it is on the body, it can be embalmed in the normal way. It could have had a PM. Let's talk about the different treatments for this kind of trauma.

If the areas will be covered in the coffin then these can be treated with cavity fluid, covered, and then wrapped in bandages. If it is the face and hands that are burnt, then the degree of the burn must be considered; if intact, then a 'new skin' spray can be applied. After that, mortuary cosmetics can be applied. No make-up will adhere to a wet surface. It must be dry. If there are blisters, they must be broken and the loose skin gently removed; the area must then be dried and 'new skin' applied.

Deep burns

Deep burns can sometimes make it impossible for the embalmer to restore and if this is the case, then hypodermic treatment should be carried out. So long as the whole body is saturated with cavity fluid and 'wrapped' there will be no odours, for this is a major problem with burnt flesh and it must be removed. At times when large amounts of a chemical have to be used externally, the embalmer is advised to wear a respirator.

External cancers

Skin cancers will begin to decompose very quickly after death. They can be injected with cavity fluid. If the cancer is on the face, then, with the family's permission, it can be removed. How is it done? Remove to skin level, dry the area by injecting a suitable chemical, then apply a thin coat of wax and cover with make-up; there are all kinds of sealants and waxes to assist you. Get the fact sheets and read up!

Strokes

If someone has died from a stroke the face may be discoloured; this is because of the haemorrhage in the brain. Injecting the carotids and drainage from the jugular vein should clear the face. Think about what I wrote earlier; the stroke may have damaged the brain's arterial system so much that your embalming fluid will not be 'carried' to it. Do you know what to do? Don't worry, I'll tell you.

Insert a small trocar (these come in varying sizes) through the nostril; it must pass through into the vault of the skull (it doesn't need to be 'rammed' in). Aspirate the cavity and then inject through the trocar about 3onz of cavity fluid. I know that the operation can sound quite gruesome, but it's the only way. Put in the nostrils cotton wool till the cavity has done the 'job', then clean the nose and repack with clean cotton wool. Do not leave until you are sure that the nose is dry.

Pressure sores

Pressure sores can occur in the human body due to insufficient blood supply to the affected area, which at first turns cold and swollen. The skin becomes moist and black and will eventually break down, and decomposition will spread rapidly. I have seen bedsores so deep that the backbone has been clearly visible. This pressure sore had obviously got 'out of hand'. The smell from pressure sores like that are unforgettable. The Embalmer will need to provide the following treatment:

    a.   Use a good arterial fluid at the strength indicated by its fact sheet.

    b.   Inject around the area of the pressure sore and then pack it with an embalming paste.

    c.   Ensure that everything you have used on a body with a bad pressure sore is either disposed of or disinfect with a special mortuary disinfectant.

Oedema

This is a collection of fluid in the tissues of the body. First, let's look at it in the limbs. If possible, the limbs should be raised above the level of the trunk. The tissue fluid will drain into the cavities, which then can be aspirated with a 'blunt-nosed' trocar; this type will not pierce any major organs.

Treating damaged skin

If the damaged skin is not on the face or hands, then it will not cause too much of a problem. If it is a laceration, tiny vessels will leak as you are embalming; the area needs to be 'dried' and then waxed. If the wound is deep, it will have to be dried by injecting a 'drying' chemical into it and then filled with a wound filler. Glues can also be used instead of sutures. However, if the wound is on the face and deep, and you want to have a go at suturing, then you can always use the intra-dermal stitch. This means suturing just under the top of the skin and pulling the edges together. You can then camouflage with wax. I used to practice on chicken skin; believe me, it's a good way to perfect your suturing.

Skin slip

Frail skin will 'slip' if the body is not handled with care. It is very unsightly and at times unnecessary. It is true, however, that after death decomposition of the body begins and the skin will begin to break down, but skin tearing can be caused by rough handling.

If the skin is blistered these must be drained and the loose skin gently removed, and a cauterant applied. Then, after you have embalmed, the area can be dried and cosmotised.

Urinary catheters

Urinary catheters must be removed from the body after embalming. These cannot be yanked out. At the external end of the tube is a small appendage; this must be snipped off to allow sterile water to escape. Once this is done, by placing a hand over the bladder and applying a little pressure, the tube will 'slip' out. Dispose of catheter and any urine that you have collected.

Stoma

A stoma is any opening on the surface of the body. If it is the intestines there will be a clear plastic bag over the opening to collect intestinal contents. This bag is best left in place until after embalming, the reason being that any contents such as faeces will be in the bag and not all over the table. Once the body has been embalmed, then the bag can be removed 'carefully'. The stoma must then be cleaned and a purse string sutured; this will close the stoma. Incinerate the bag.

Intravenous tubes

These can be removed after embalming. There should only be the canulas left in, but be warned—sometimes needles are left in. Take care and afterwards seal puncture marks with wax. Dispose of any needles in a special 'sharps box'.

Post mortem changes in the human body

I have frequently referred to decomposition in this book. I will now go through the stages of it.

Changes that bring about decomposition are caused by the actions of the body itself. We carry friendly bacteria on and inside our bodies during life, but once we die they will begin to ingest the body to its eventual destruction. One of the first signs is a greenish tinge just over the lower right of the abdomen. This is where it begins. The natural bacteria that we have in our gut begins to migrate from the area and cause decomposition. You will be able to tell approximately how long a body has been dead by the extent of the colour. Of course, this is a sure sign of death.

Hypostasis

Don't let this word worry you—it only means that the blood in the body has fallen by gravity to the lowest part. For instance, if the body died on its back then you would see the purple discoloration along the bottom half of the body; however, if the subject died lying on the face, that too will be discoloured and, depending on how long the body has been on its face could be a problem. If the blood is allowed to remain 'static' it can permanently stain the tissues. Then hypostasis becomes 'haemolysis'—which is permanent. Embalming via the circulatory system will not clear it if it is severe, but there are chemicals that will bleach it out.

Rigor mortis/death stiffening

Rigor mortis affects all the muscles of the body after death. The onset and duration is of no concern to me, so let's get on with its process and how to deal with it. Commencing in the neck and jaw, it will go up to the face and then spread downwards to the rest of the body. It needs to be broken down, and this is done by passive movements of the limbs.

In young adults it can be quite hard to break down; in babies and young children it will be easy; in old people it will be even easier, so it must be done with care or you will break bones! You may have read that rigor mortis, if not broken down, will prevent the fluid reaching the tissue. Although I am all for breaking it down, the limbs in a young fit body can sometimes be impossible to move, so leave it. There is no use giving yourself a hernia; if there is someone to help, then by all means get them to do it. But I have nearly always worked alone and I have had to leave it. But my body embalmed well. A word of advice—if you ever have to embalm a body that has just died, rigor mortis may not be apparent. But the body must be placed in a relaxed position. The hands must be placed at the side of the body and the features must be set. This is because bodies that have just died tend to fix their position quickly, so make sure it looks right.

Suturing

The needle is a dangerous instrument. Inserting a needle, be it hand-held or in a syringe, can prick! And the problem is that once the needle has been in the skin of a corpse there will be tissue on the end of it! We can't see it, so if you prick yourself you must remove your glove and encourage the puncture to bleed under running water; then it must be treated with a suitable disinfectant and covered. Get rid of the gloves and put on a fresh pair.

Now we can get on with the 'mouth suture'. A curved needle is loaded with suture and passed through the tissue close to the bottom teeth. It is then passed through again, but not through the same holes. Then the needle is passed up and behind the top lip and through the nostril and passed through the nose septum. At the other side it is passed down through the nostril behind the top lip and out the two ends of the ligature, then tied to set the mouth. You will need a little practice with this, but it isn't hard.

Now let's say that the tissue in front of the bottom teeth is not firm enough to hold the suture; no good struggling, it will not hold, so you can take the needle and push it between the lower lip and gum. It will appear through the skin at the point of the chin. Turn the needle and enter through the hole you have just made and bring it up through the floor of the mouth under the tongue. Then carry on as before. If this fails—and it can—there are glues that can be used.

Observations on Instruments and Equipment

The trocar

Another lethal instrument. Used to puncture organs and deliver chemicals into the body. The trocar is a must in your embalming kit. One large and one small. It must be kept scrupulously clean or it will fail you when you need it most.

The pump

This will have to be serviced regularly. It is this that pumps the fluid around. Personally, I use a hand pump to inject my fluid, but need the machine for aspiration. I hate using hand pumps for taking fluids out; they are too time-consuming and dammed hard work.

As with all embalming instruments, you will need to know the best way to clean and store them. Never use household bleach—it has no place in the mortuary. There are special disinfectants in which to soak your instruments, after which they must be thoroughly dried and stored in a dry container. Sharps must always be stored separately, and if they are disposable, put them in a 'sharps box'. Never leave a mortuary dirty and refuse to work in one that is. I have worked in many unsuitable conditions as part of my learning process, but I would never subject any student to unsuitable conditions. Before leaving the mortuary you must check the sluice. Is it clean? Check the table. Is it clean? Check all jars—are they clean? Is the floor clean? Are all instruments clean? It doesn't take long, but bad habits are easy to fall into and hard to get out of.

Facial Matters

The hair

Caring for the hair makes a lot of difference to the finished 'job' and in some cases you don't have to wash it. You can use a dry shampoo and then style it (Ask for a photo). One of the things that really annoys me is when I see a body in its coffin and the hair is swept back, no effort having been made to style it!

Beards

Never shave a beard off because you don't like it. Always ask if it needs to be left on or not, but always tidy it up if need be.

Facial hair on women

Look closely at the facial hair of a woman. If there is any stubble, then she will have shaved in life. If the hair is long, leave it.

Make-up

Not all women wear make up. I remember too well a young woman I embalmed. She had a lovely face, and I put make-up on her. I thought she looked so nice, and so did the funeral director, but the family ordered it off. So beware. For obvious reasons, there are times when we do have to apply make-up, but never use the sort from the High Street—it must be mortuary make-up. And be as discreet as you can.

A Guide to Finding Organs

The heart needs to be drained of its blood, even after Venus drainage. The simplest way to got into the heart is to make an incision near the navel. Take a trocar and push it in the direction of the right earlobe. Now you're all set to go through the muscle called the diaphragm. You are not going all the way to the right ear, of course—this is just a path line. The right atrium lies usually under and between the fourth and fifth rib, and once the diaphragm gives in to your trocar, pull slightly back and you should pierce the right atrium. This needs a lot of practice, but once you get the feel of it, it becomes easy. Please do not rush this operation—take your time.

The stomach

Should you wish to aspirate the stomach, then you need to point the trocar to the level of the fifth rib on the left side of the body.

The bladder

The tip of the trocar should just be pushed under the pubic bone. Do not go too deep. If the bladder is full it will be high towards the top of the pubis and will easily give up its contents. A word of warning. Bodies that have died from kidney failure may have a high content of fluid in the abdominal area; the fluid will contain ammonia and ammonia neutralizes formaldehyde, so make sure you remove it with a blunt nosed trocar before embalming.

Before Embalming

Before embalming we have to check important documents.

1.   the family must have registered the death

2.   if it is a cremation the body has to be examined by two doctors

3.   family must have given their consent to embalming

4.   not every family wants this service, so respect their wishes

Your protective clothing

- Theatre gown
- Waterproof plastic pinafore long enough to go over boots
- Rubber gloves
- Waterproof arm sleeves
- Goggles

Test for death

- Touch the centre of the eye with soft cotton wool; if there is no reaction, the subject is brain dead (nervous system).
- Place a mirror in front of the mouth; if it doesn't mist up the subject is not breathing (respiratory system).
- Feel the carotid artery; if you can't feel a pulse, then the heart has stopped (circulatory system).

You have just convinced yourself that the subject is dead

The body

After checking I.D. remove any jewellery and put in a safe place. Put a modesty cloth over the private parts and remove any clothing. Break down rigor mortis and wash the body. Look for signs that will tell you how best to embalm. Remove dentures or clean teeth and wash mouth. Clean eyes and nose. The mouth can be sutured at this stage or not, but if it is not, tie off—just tie a bow in case you have to clear the throat. Check orifices for packing and remove them; they will have to be replaced with clean ones later.

Useful tips

Here are some useful tips you can try when you are embalming:

1) Clingfilm

This is ideal for areas you have treated and covered. Wrap around and secure. This film will prevent leaks. It can also be used with a spray adhesive to cover trunk incisions. First spray along incision with adhesive, then place a strip of wadding over the top, not too thick; then spray up to the clingfilm so that it covers the wadding but wide enough to adhere to the skin.

2) Plastic sheeting

Plastic sheeting is good for bodies that have pressure sores, but you may need help getting the plastic under the body. It needs to be long enough to go up to the armpits and wide enough to wrap around the body, and long enough to reach the back of the knees. Look at the size of the body—the sheet must be 'a good square'. Now the legs must be splayed and the plastic sheet cut. Take a pair of scissors and run them along the inside of each leg till you can go no further; now you will have a piece of plastic that you can pull up to the trunk. (It should look like a nappy.) Glue it to the skin, then take one side of the sheet and spray it and fold it over the body. Do the same with the other side. Not only will it look neat (after a few tries) but it will make the body easier to manoeuvre.

3) Mouth adhesive

If you want to 'glue' a mouth for whatever reason, do not glue the lips; there are special mouth glues for this kind of work. Place the glue on the teeth. Make sure that the inside of the lips are dry. If it doesn't look right, then the glue will come off easily. Do not use ordinary glue. There should be instructions.

4) The head in a PM case

The top of the skull will have been removed and sometimes there can be problems with leakages from the sutures behind the ears; these will stain the 'pillow' and to prevent this, the embalmer can use an absorbent pad to push down behind the ears.

Let's say that you have finished embalming and you have changed the packing in the skull cavity; replace the top of the skull and make sure it is in the right position. Then, before you bring the scalp together, make an incision close to the skull behind the ears and slip an absorbent pad against the skull. Remember that the adhesive side of the pad is to go against the skull. Then bring the scalp together and suture. Keep your stitches close till you get a little nearer to the middle of the back of the head. Most leaks will start behind the ears; your absorbent pad will stop it. You will have to practice.

5) Mouth formers

These are useful if the body has no teeth. It can be difficult to set a mouth if the teeth have been broken or lost. They are not expensive to buy.

There are books that will take you through advanced embalming techniques but they are expensive and the reader will have to have gained enough knowledge about practical embalming even to begin to understand; once you have learnt the basics of embalming then by all means go further.

6) Long hair

It can be difficult to suture the scalp if the hair of the subject is long; depending on length, styling mousse will hold the hair away from the cut edges of the scalp; and, of course, if the hair is very long, then hair grips can be used to hold the hair away from the scalp incision. You must not try to take up pieces of hair whilst suturing. And always do small sutures when you start behind the ears; they can become a little more spaced out as you get to the middle.

Remember, leaks on the pillow are not acceptable; they are an embarrassment to the funeral director and distressing to the bereaved.

7) Massage cream

Have in your embalming kit a 3" paint brush. You can use it to apply the cream instead of using your hands. It can also be used for applying formaldehyde gels.

8) Bald patches

These can be covered by taking pieces of hair from the back of the subject's head and sticking into place.

9) Pacemaker

This must be removed before embalming. Usually in the upper chest area. It will be under the skin and can easily be 'felt' after making an incision above its length. The pacemaker will slide out; there will be a wire attached, so gently pull out pacemaker and snip off the wire.

10) Vein tubes

A little massage cream smeared over the end will assist tube into vein.

11) White hair

Talcum powder brushed through white hair makes it appear thicker.

12) Chiffon scarf

Placed over head, this will prevent make-up coming into contact with clothing (ladies).

13) Chemicals for specific conditions

For all the following conditions you will be able to buy a chemical to deal with them:

1. Unbroken skin.

2. Bed sores

3. Drowning

4. Dehydrated tissues

5. Incisions

6. Severe injury cases

7. Jaundice

8. Oedema

9. Complexion

10. Cavities

11. Viscera

12. Superficial wounds

13. Deep wounds

14. Swollen neck

15. Mouth

16. Eyes

17. Cranium

18. Disinfectants

19. Odours

20. Decomposition

I do not advertise brand names but you would be advised to buy from an established embalming supplier.

Confusing Words Made Easy

Some embalming students are confused by medical names. But in laymen's terms they are not really acceptable in the embalming theatre, and indeed sound more professional if they are used. One example would be the 'belly button'; try not to refer to the 'umbilicus' as the 'belly button'! I will give you a list of words that you may come across whilst learning to embalm.

1. sternum = the breast plate

2. radial artery = small superficial vessel that doctors feel when taking the pulse (good for clearing hands)

3.   viscera = internal organs

4.   calavarium = top of skull

5.   hypostasis = discoloration of tissues after death

6.   heamolysis = staining of the tissue after death

7.   trachea = wind pipe

8.   oesophagus = food pipe

9.   rigor mortis = death stiffening

10. oedema = accumulation of fluid in limbs/cavities

11. hypoclorite = bleaching chemical for drains and traps

12. phenolic = chemical used for instruments

13. petichea = tiny bruises on skin

14. anterior = the front

15. posterior = the back

16. superior = above

17. inferior = bellow

18. lateral = to the side

19. median = to the middle

20. supine = body lying on back

21. skin slip = skin tear

22. adipose tissue = fat

23. sluice = for body fluids

24. autoclave = sterilizing machine for instruments

25. bulb syringe = for pumping fluid in body by hand

26. jaundice = yellow

27. C V A = cerebral vascular accident (stroke)

28. decomposition = decay

29. Crem film = white plastic sheeting

Conclusion

I hope you've found 'Caring for the Dead' helpful. The decision to become an embalmer is not to be taken lightly. You will have to follow the rules. Embalming is an honourable art that demands the best from those who practice it. Families entrust their loved ones into our hands, and so we have to be an extension of the care they received in life. Death has no respect for age or gender, and you will be taken to the limits with some of the cases that you 'care for'. At times the experience can be harrowing, but give it your best to satisfy yourself that with your skill and understanding of those bereaved you and you alone have made it possible for someone to say their last goodbyes in peace.

My website will soon be up and running for practical embalming advice. More information will be found at www.diadembooks.com/embalming.htm

The Author

Josephine Price Powell was born January 27th, 1943, in the Lancashire Dock area. Her father was a merchant seaman and her mother a housewife. The youngest of five children, she had two brothers and two sisters, one of whom she called 'little mother'. Expelled from school at 14 for refusing to 'work', she travelled with horse dealers.

Her love for horses landed her a job teaching children to ride. When she grew out of horses at the age of 19, she ended up on the dole, pregnant at 25. Needing money to support her baby, she began a singing career which took her to the Royal Albert Hall in London.

Homesick for Lancashire, she returned to her old haunts and was advised to 'change direction' and go into the funeral profession—and so became an embalmer 'working and caring' for the dead.

She decided to write a book after being asked so many times about the Art of Embalming and how she got into it.

Jo Powell has seen Death many times, through the eyes of a child, a woman and an embalmer. She understands the needs of those wishing to become embalmers and the difficulties that face them. Her book tells of her encounters with the Dead and how to care for them in a way that can easily be understood by the reader.

Further information about Jo Powell and her book will be found at
www.diadembooks.com/embalming.htm

Notes

Notes

Notes

Notes

Notes

Notes